ADVANCED BASS FISHING

THE HUNTING & FISHING LIBRARY®

By Dick Sternberg

DICK STERNBERG, a nationally known multispecies angler, has authored 15 books in the Hunting & Fishing Library series. One of his favorite pastimes is light-tackle fishing for smallmouth bass.

JIM MOYNAGH is a former Minnesota B.A.S.S. Federation champion and twice represented the state in the Wrangler/B.A.S.S. National Championship. He is a University of Minnesota Fisheries graduate.

CY DECOSSE INCORPORATED

Creative Publishing

A Division of Cowles Enthusiast Media, Inc.

President/COO: Nino Tarantino
Executive V. P./Editor-in-Chief: William B. Jones

ADVANCED BASS FISHING

Author and Project Director: Dick Sternberg
Book Development Leader and Technical Advisor: Jim Moynagh
Editor: Janice Cauley
Project Manager: John van Vliet
Senior Art Directors: Dave Schelitzche, Bradley Springer
Art Directors: Kathlynn Henthorne, Gina Seeling
Researchers: Steve Hauge, Mike Hehner, Andy Lessin, Jim Moynagh
Creative Photo Coordinator: Cathleen Shannon
Director of Photography: Mike Parker
Studio Manager: Marcia Chambers
Principal Photographers: Mike Hehner, William Lindner
Staff Photographers: Rebecca Hawthorne, Mark Macemon, Charles Nields
Contributing Photographers: California Dept. of Fish and Game; Gerald Crawford – B.A.S.S. Inc.; Andy Lessin; Jim Moynagh; Susan Grigsby Powers; David Sams; Dick Sternberg
Photo Assistants: Steve Hauge, Mike Hehner, Andy Lessin, Jim Moynagh, John van Vliet
V.P. Development, Planning and Production: Jim Bindas
Production Manager: Laurie Gilbert
Senior Desktop Publishing Specialist: Joe Fahey
Production Staff: Amy Berndt, John Hermanson, Elaine Johnson, Mike Schauer, Nik Wogstad
Illustrators: Thomas Boll, Dave Schelitzche

Enthusiast Media

President/COO: Philip L. Penny

Contributing Manufacturers: ABU Garcia; Fred Arbogast Company, Inc.; B.A.S.S.; Berkley Inc.; Better Fishing Ways Company; Blakemore Lure Co.; Charlie Brewer's Slider Company, Inc.; Carlson Tackle Company; Daiwa Corporation; Do-It Lure and Sinker Molds; Evinrude Outboards; Fenwick; Fleck Lure Company; Gitzit Inc./Bass'n Man Lures; Granite State Bass Baits; Harrison Hoge Industries, Inc.; Hart Tackle Company, Inc.; Hobie Sunglasses; Jerry's Jigs; J-Mac Lures Corp.; Johnson Outboards; Kalin Company; Lake Systems; Luck "E" Strike U.S.A.; Lund Boat Company; Lunker City; Mann's Bait Company; Mercury Marine; Minn Kota

Electric Fishing Motors; Mojo Lures; Normark Corporation; Operation Bass; Plano Molding Company; Poe's Lures/Yakima Bait Company; Pradco; Stanley Jigs, Inc.; Storm Manufacturing Company; Stowaway Marine Batteries; Stratos Boats, Inc.; Strike King Lure Company; Uncle Josh Bait Company; VMC Inc.; Gary Yamamoto Custom Baits; Zoomer Products

Cooperating Agencies and Individuals: Apache Lake Marina and Resort; Arizona Game and Fish Dept. – Jim Warnecke; Arizona Office of Tourism; British Columbia Ministry of Environment, Lands and Parks – Peter Newroth; California Dept. of Fish and Game – Jim Adams, Dennis Fiedler; Terry Foreman, Dennis Lee, Dwayne Maxwell, Ivan Paulsen, Steve Taylor; Comfort Inn; Dan Foote; John Hale; Homer Humphreys; Robert Jenkins; Keith Kline; David Klossner; Katherine Landing; Los Angeles County Dept. of Parks and Recreation – Brian Roney; Minnesota Dept. of Natural Resources – Chip Welling; Bill Murphy; New Hampshire Fish and Game Dept.; Oak Ridge Resort; Pauls Valley Chamber of Commerce; Rayburn Country Resort; Roosevelt Lake Resort; Bill Ross; City of San Diego Dept. of Water Utilities – Larry Bottroff, Jim Brown; Silver Sands Motel; Texas Parks and Wildlife Dept. – David Campbell, Barry Lyons; Joe Thrun; Western Outdoor News – Bud Neville, Bill Rice

Printed on American paper by: R. R. Donnelley & Sons Co.

99 98 97 96 / 5 4 3 2 1

Copyright © 1995 by Cy DeCosse Incorporated
5900 Green Oak Drive
Minnetonka, MN 55343
1-800-328-3895

Library of Congress - Cataloging-in-Publication Data
Sternberg, Dick.-
Advanced bass fishing / by Dick Sternberg
p. cm. – (The Hunting & fishing library)
Includes index. ISBN 0-86573-041-5
1. Bass fishing. I. Title. II. Series.
SH681.S73 1995   94-36044
799.1′758 – dc20

Contents

Introduction

With the explosion of interest in tournament fishing in recent years, bass-fishing methodology and equipment is evolving at an unprecedented rate. *Advanced Bass Fishing* focuses on the latest bass-fishing innovations, but also includes many refinements of techniques that have been around for a long time.

As a first step in planning this book, our editors surveyed the professional bass-fishing world to determine the newest and best techniques to feature. Then, they looked through the pro bass ranks to see who could best explain and demonstrate the techniques to our readers.

Many top-name pros were chosen to demonstrate the particular technique with which they're most closely associated. For instance, Ken Cook, a former BASS Masters Classic champion, is widely known for his spinnerbait expertise, so he was selected for "Spinnerbaiting the Wood." His technique, like all of the others, was carefully dissected to give you the kind of detail left out of most other books and magazine articles. It is this detail that separates the real professionals from the want-to-bes.

However, not every featured expert is a top-name pro. Some were chosen strictly for their expertise on a very specific type of fishing. Minnesota's Pat Martin, for instance, is not a widely known name in tournament-fishing circles. But he helped perfect the technique demonstrated in "Yo-yoing for Bass in Dense Milfoil."

Once a pro was selected, our staff traveled to a site of his choosing to witness the technique first-hand. The pro explained all of the technique's intricacies, and we photographed every aspect of it in step-by-step detail.

The book is organized into four main chapters according to lure type, including soft plastics, jigs, plugs and spinnerbaits. Every chapter includes three to four sections outlining different techniques. Besides providing detailed information on tackle and presentation, each gives you when-and-where recommendations, and a collection of the pros' personal tips – the little things they do to get an edge on the competition.

Another chapter is devoted entirely to tournament fishing. We walk you through the procedures you need to follow to become a successful tournament angler, from pretournament research, to prefishing tactics to tournament-day strategies, which vary greatly depending on the type of tournament you enter. As an added bonus, this chapter includes the personal tournament-fishing philosophies of some of the country's top pros.

Scattered throughout the book are sidebars that present information only marginally related to the technique, but of great interest to many anglers. In the section, "Football Jigs: Magic for Pre-spawn Bass," for example, we'll show you how to de-gas bass brought up from deep water, greatly increasing the survival rate of those you release.

Despite the book's high level of detail and focus on professional bass-fishing tactics, it is a valuable resource for all bass anglers. By looking beyond the basics, a novice can learn quickly and develop a feel for what's necessary to consistently outwit bass.

Advanced Soft-Plastic Techniques

Shaw's Sight-Fishing Secrets

Most veteran bass anglers cringe at the thought of fishing a clear lake on a calm, sunny day. The bass are either holding so tight to cover or hugging so tight to the bottom that you can't see them on a graph. And even if you do locate some fish, getting them to bite is a real challenge.

Optimal Conditions:

Type of Water: any clear body of water
Season: spring through fall
Water Temperature: doesn't matter, as long as bass are in the shallows
Weather: calm, sunny
Water Stage: any stage
Water Depth: depends on clarity
Water Clarity: 3 feet or more
Time of Day: mid-morning to late afternoon

But Shaw Grigsby, the famed bass pro from Gainesville, Florida, seldom has a problem finding bass – he simply goes out and looks for them. While scouting, he may do some blind casting, but his foremost intent is spotting fish, or subtle signs of their presence, such as fin movement, vague shapes and shadows. Then he makes precise casts to catch the fish he sees.

This may sound like a remarkably easy way to locate bass, but it's really not. "Most people I fish with don't see 'em," Grigsby says. "They're not really sight fishing, they're looking for something in the water to throw at. Even when I take them by the hand and tell them to look right there, they still don't see 'em.

"But once you learn to spot the fish, there's nothing like it. You know the fish are there, so you don't waste time in unproductive water or in areas that hold only small ones. And it's an adrenaline rush to watch the fish – how he takes the bait and how he handles it in his mouth."

Shaw Grigsby

Hometown:
Gainesville, Florida
Favorite Waters for Technique:
Sam Rayburn Lake, Texas; Lake Ontario, New York
Career Highlights:
Ranks fourth on B.A.S.S. all-time money list
Winner: 1984 Red Man All-American Championship; Texas BASSMASTER Invitational (3 times); 1993 Georgia BASSMASTER BP Top 100
Qualified for BASS Masters Classic 6 out of 7 years from 1988 to 1994

Clear, calm water is best for sight fishing

When and Where to Sight-Fish

Sight fishing obviously requires clear water. As a rule, don't try to sight-fish where you can't see the bottom.

For maximum visibility, the surface should be calm, the skies clear and the sun directly overhead. You won't see much on a breezy day because of the ripples, and cloud cover makes it harder to see detail. When the sun is at a low angle, much of the light reflects off the surface, rather than penetrating the water to illuminate the bottom.

If possible, do your sight fishing along a protected bank. Even a barely perceptible breeze creates enough surface disturbance to obscure visibility along a bank that is exposed to the wind.

You can sight-fish whenever bass are in the shallows, which could be from the pre-spawn period well into fall. In late fall, however, when the water temperature in the shallows drops below that in the depths, most of the bass head for deeper water. In the South, the critical fall water temperature is 55 to 60°F; in the North, 45 to 50°F.

How to Spot Bass Under Poor Sight-fishing Conditions

CAST into areas where the reflection from the shoreline darkens the water whenever glare is a problem.

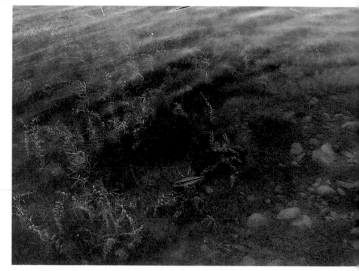
LOOK for bass along the inside weed edge in waters that are too weedy or murky for good sight fishing. This inner zone is usually clearer and weed-free.

The best time to find bass in the shallows is after a few warm, sunny days in early spring. Bass move out of the main water body, which is still very cold, into shallow bays, coves or creek arms, which are a little warmer. And most of the fish are cruising, looking for food and spawning sites, so they're easy to see. Cold fronts drive fish out of the shallows, or they bury themselves in thick cover, where they can't be seen.

In reservoirs with shad populations, bass commonly herd the baitfish into the back ends of coves and creek arms in fall. The clearest creek arms are generally those nearest the dam. Try sight fishing in these areas if you see circling gulls or other bird activity, or lots of shad flipping on the surface.

Sight fishing is difficult in water deeper than ten feet, even if the clarity is adequate. Unless the surface is perfectly calm, which is rarely the case, distortion prevents you from clearly seeing the fish.

Dense bottom cover also reduces sight-fishing possibilities. It's easy to spot fish around rocks or fallen trees or even in brush piles, but not in a lush weedbed.

CHECK isolated bays that do not receive runoff when the main water body is too muddy.

Nest-robbers quickly move in when a nest-guarding bass is removed

Angling for Spawners: An Ongoing Controversy

Sight fishing can be deadly in spring, when bass congregate in the shallows to spawn. Often, the fish are protecting a nest and refuse to leave, even with a boat hovering overhead. If they do leave, they usually return a few minutes later.

Although nest-guarding bass can be extremely finicky, you can generally irritate them into striking by dabbling a tube bait or worm, or some type of live bait, in the spawning bed. In Florida, more than half of all trophy bass are taken during the spawning period, mainly by bobber-fishing with big golden shiners. Waterdogs, leeches and nightcrawlers also work well for nest-guarding bass.

Anglers and fisheries managers have long debated the subject of fishing during the spawning period. At present, only five northern states totally prohibit fishing around spawning time. Thirty-five states, mainly in the South, have year-round seasons. The remainder allow year-round fishing, but have special size limits, bag limits or catch-and-release regulations to control harvest.

Closed seasons appear to be justified in the North, where rapidly warming temperatures in the spring tend to compress the spawning season. Nest building, spawning and guarding of fry may all take place in a

month or less, meaning all individuals that are going to spawn are doing so at about the same time. Because the fish are tightly concentrated in the shallows, they're extremely vulnerable to angling.

Several northern states have recently changed their regulations to allow catch-and-release fishing at spawning time. Some biologists, however, question whether a bass caught off the nest will return in time to protect it from predators. Studies are presently being conducted to answer this question. Other biologists maintain that it really makes no difference if the fish return to their nests in time, because it only takes a few successful nests to provide an adequate number of fry.

Fishing for bass during the spawning period is an age-old tradition in the South, and there seems to be little reason to change. Because the water temperature stays considerably warmer in winter, the spring warm-up is much more gradual, and the spawning period is greatly extended. A few fish spawn early and then leave, while others continue to trickle in, some as much as four months later. Consequently, spawning concentrations are lighter than in the North, lessening the need for protection.

Sight-Fishing Techniques

The major challenge in sight fishing is to spot the fish before it spots you. Otherwise, it will usually dart toward deeper water, and even if it doesn't, it will probably refuse your lure.

To minimize spooking, stand in the bow and move along with your troll motor. Wear drab clothing and be sure to avoid reds, yellows and whites. While blind casting with a minnow plug or soft stickbait, look as far ahead of the boat as possible. Move fast enough to cover a good deal of water, but not so fast that your momentum carries you over the fish. The easier it is to see them, the faster you can go. Always wear polarized sunglasses and try to keep the sun at your back so glare will not prevent you from seeing into the water.

When you see a bass, immediately reverse direction, switch to another rod rigged with a tube bait and cast to the fish before it sees you. Keep a low profile, stay far enough away from the fish that you can barely see it and don't make any sudden movements or unnecessary noises.

Bass in clear water tend to be superalert and not as aggressive as those in murky water. This explains why Grigsby prefers a tube bait. "It looks natural,

and you can swim it like a minnow or slow-crawl it like a crayfish," he says.

Grigsby recommends injection-molded, rather than hand-dipped, tube baits. The hand-dipped models may look a little nicer, but the injection-molded type is bulkier, heavier and softer. The weight and bulkiness make it easy to skip-cast (below), and the softness means a bass will hold onto it longer.

The way the bait sinks also makes a difference. "When a baitfish dies, it spirals down," Grigsby points out. "I've found that a bait that does the same is much more effective than one that plummets straight down." An ordinary bullet sinker would not give the bait this spiraling action, so Grigsby rigs his baits with a special hook and internal weight he helped design. A clip on the hook secures the bait, and the weight (below) gives it the desired action.

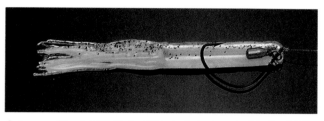

Cutaway of Luck "E" Strike G4 tube bait rigged with size 1 HP hook and internal weight

He normally uses a 1/16-ounce weight, but when it's windy or he wants to keep the bait on bottom to mimic a crayfish, he switches to a 1/8-ounce.

Don't cast right to the fish, or it may spook. If it's motionless, cast well past it and draw the bait 3 to 5 feet in front of it. If it's swimming, lead it accordingly. A skip-cast is best, because it mimics a skittering baitfish. Skip-casting these light lures is easiest with a spinning outfit, preferably with a long-spool reel, and light mono, no more than 8-pound test. A high gear ratio, at least 5:1, enables you to reel in quickly and cast to another fish you've sighted.

How to Sight Fish

LOOK for bass while moving along and blind casting.

SKIP-CAST ahead of a fish you've spotted.

SELECT the color of your polarized sunglasses based on light conditions. Compared to an unpolarized view (left), brown lenses (middle) enable you to spot fish better on a sunny day; yellow lenses (right) on a cloudy day. Blue lenses, or the gray ones used by most anglers, do not provide as much contrast.

Sometimes the fish will strike as soon as the bait hits the water, or it may grab the bait as it's spiraling down. But the vast majority of strikes come in response to an excruciatingly slow retrieve, accomplished by moving the rod tip no more than an inch at a time to crawl the bait along the bottom. Or, try barely jiggling the bait without moving it ahead.

After watching a few fish react to your bait, you'll learn to judge their catchability. If a fish bolts away or shows no response to the bait, keep moving, and try to find new fish. One that turns on the bait and tips down to inspect it, however, can probably be caught. Keep casting as long as it shows interest.

If the fish just keeps following, twitch the bait sharply to mimic a scooting crayfish; this last-ditch maneuver may draw a reflex strike.

You may have to change baits, sometimes more than once, to draw a strike. Try a small plastic crawfish or, when fishing for spawners, a 5-inch lizard. In fall, when fish are feeding on shad, a 4-inch ringworm is a good option.

There's no way to avoid spooking some fish as you motor through the shallows. But the fish that move away usually don't go far. Remember exactly where you saw them and come back a little later. Knowing where they are, you should be able to get within casting range without alarming them.

When you see a fish take the bait or feel a strike, reel down until your rod points at the fish, then pull back with a smooth sweep. The light-wire hook penetrates easily, so there is no need to risk snapping the line with a full-power hook set.

If it's obvious that you won't be able to keep the fish from swimming into a brush pile or around a dock pole, don't keep fighting it or it will wrap your line around the cover. Instead, back off on the tension and let it swim freely. After it stops running, try to ease it back out of the cover the same way it went in. The method is not foolproof, but it's the best way to land fish on light line.

Sight fishing has helped Grigsby claim numerous major tournament titles, including three wins in the Texas BASSMASTER Invitational, an unprecedented accomplishment. But there are other reasons he enjoys sight fishing. "It's highly intense," he explains. "You're one-on-one with the fish – it's totally you against him. And that's what does it for me."

CRAWL the bait just ahead of the bass.

JIGGLE, then pause, to draw a strike.

SCOOT the bait to mimic a crayfish.

Draggin': Refinement of a Time-Proven Method

Optimal Conditions:
Type of Water: weedy reservoirs that are drawn down in fall and rise in spring
Season: spring
Water Temperature: low 50s to 70°F
Cover Type: clean to sparsely vegetated bottom
Water Stage: high
Water Depth: 5 to 15 feet
Water Clarity: at least 1 foot
Time of Day: anytime

In East Texas, it's called "draggin'" – most everywhere else, it's Carolina rigging. The technique originated in South Carolina decades ago, but never gained widespread popularity until Jim Nolan used it to claim the 1991 Texas BASSMASTER BP Top 100 tournament on Sam Rayburn Lake. Most of his record-breaking catch of 86 pounds, 6 ounces was taken on a Carolina-rigged lizard.

With the new soft plastics now available, draggin' is more effective than ever. According to Jay Yelas, one of pro bass fishing's elite, "There's no better way to put a quick limit in the boat. It's one of the simplest and surest ways to catch numbers of bass."

A Carolina rig differs from a Texas rig in that the bullet sinker is positioned well up the line (p. 18), rather than riding on the nose of the bait. This way, the bait sinks much more slowly and has a more enticing action. With a Texas rig, the hook is always buried in the bait; with a Carolina rig, it may or may not be, depending on density of the cover. Texas fishermen have dubbed this technique draggin' because all you do is cast out and drag the bait in with short pulls.

Originally, a Carolina rig consisted of an egg sinker, a barrel swivel and an ordinary worm hook. Yelas modifies the rig somewhat by substituting a bullet sinker for the egg sinker and a wide-bend, locking-style hook for the standard worm hook. He adds a

glass bead to prevent the sinker from damaging the knot on the swivel.

Yelas prefers a heavy bullet sinker, about 1 ounce. This much weight enables long casts, helps you "read" the bottom, and lets you fish practically any water depth. It also gets the bait to the bottom quickly and keeps it there, even on a fairly rapid retrieve or from a moving boat. As a result, you can cover more water in a given time than you could with a lighter Texas rig. The sinker may also attract bass by kicking up silt on the bottom and clicking against the glass bead.

Yelas, winner of the 1993 Maryland BASSMASTER BP Top 100 tournament on the Potomac River, always has one rod set up with a draggin' rig in tournament competition, and the technique has contributed to several of his high finishes.

Jay Yelas

Hometown:
Sam Rayburn, Texas
Favorite Waters for Technique:
Sam Rayburn Lake, Texas; Lake Seminole, Georgia/Florida; Lake Guntersville, Alabama
Career Highlights:
Winner: 1989 Red Man Tournament of Champions; 1993 Maryland BASSMASTER BP Top 100
3rd place 1993 BASS Masters Classic

Best Conditions for Draggin'

Yelas uses some variation of this technique throughout the year and in a wide variety of waters, but he relies on it most heavily in spring, from the pre-spawn through the post-spawn period. "Bass can be real fussy around spawning time," he says, "so they're more likely to grab a slow-sinking bait." Draggin' also has an edge over most other techniques in calm, sunny weather, for the same reason.

Draggin' works best on a clean to sparsely vegetated bottom. It is not recommended for use in heavy vegetation or woody cover; the unweighted bait will not penetrate the cover as well as a Texas rig or a leadhead jig.

Yelas contends that the very best situation for draggin' is in a reservoir that is routinely drawn down in fall. The weeds, usually hydrilla, milfoil or peppergrass, die off on structure exposed by the drawdown,

and, when the lake refills in spring, many shallow points and bars are weed-free (below and opposite). "If you know how far the lake was drawn down, you know where the inside weedline will be," Yelas explains. "The depth of the weedline is the same all over the lake. You fish the clean-bottomed structure from the weedline on in, or the fringe of the weeds."

In early spring, before spawning begins, look for clean Vs (opposite) in the back ends of creek arms. The weedline of these Vs holds fish throughout the day, but the action is fastest in late afternoon, because of the warming water.

Around spawning time, you'll still find some bass along the weedlines, but most of them have moved into shallower bushes, where they will nest. Work the weedlines in the morning, but move to the bushes on a sunny afternoon, because the warming water draws females into the shallows. When the bass are bedding, a tube jig, a floating minnow plug or an unweighted lizard usually works better than a Carolina rig.

Once spawning is completed, a few stragglers remain in the spawning areas, but you'll find most bass on points, humps and flats closer to or in the main lake. Start fishing inside weedlines on these spots in the morning. Later in the day, you'll also find bass in deeper bushes, especially when the water is high.

Because this technique relies mainly on visual attraction, it's most effective where the water is fairly clear. The visibility should be at least one foot and preferably two or more. In murkier water, a noisier bait, such as a spinnerbait, would be a better choice than a Carolina rig.

How the Inside Weedline Forms in a Reservoir

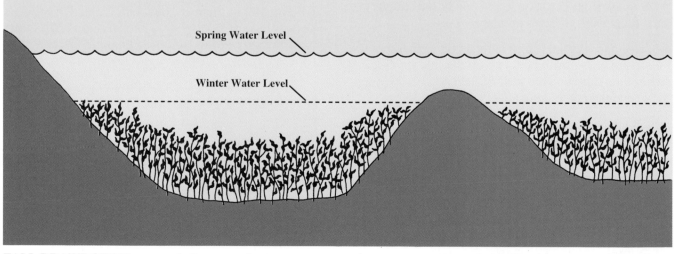

FALL DRAWDOWNS expose shallow, weedy structure, causing the vegetation to die. Weeds remain in areas still covered by water. When the water level rises in spring, bare spots remain on the shallow structure, and the adjacent deeper areas are heavily vegetated. Weeds develop on the shallow areas as the season progresses.

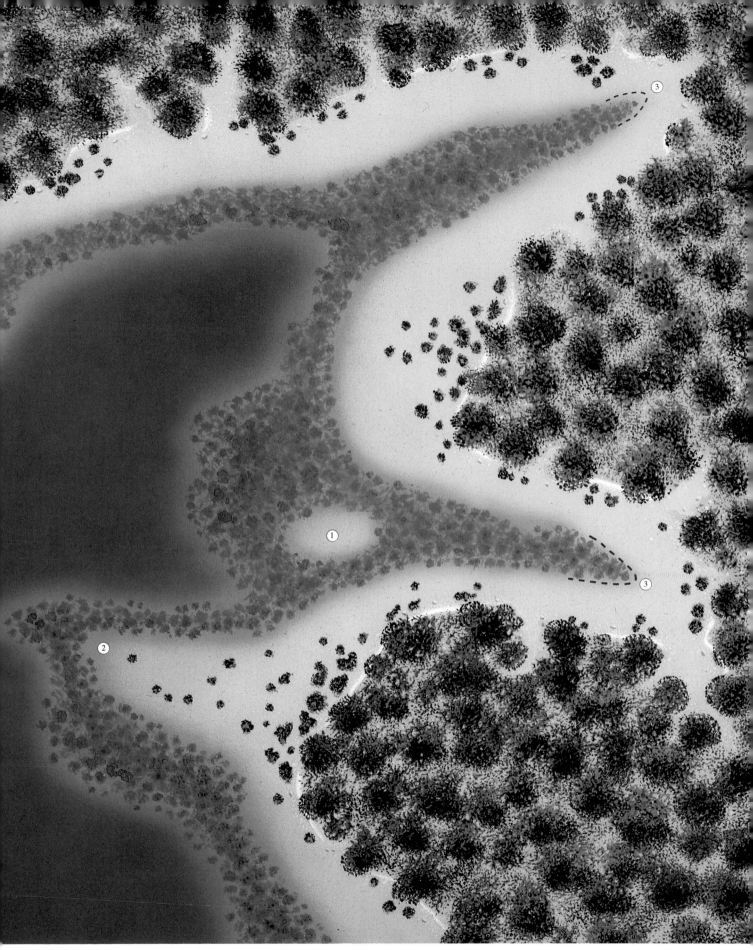

LOOK for bass where the fall drawdown creates shallow bare spots with deeper weeds nearby. Prime locations include (1) shallow humps, (2) points and (3) clean Vs (dotted line) in the back ends of coves and creek arms.

The Draggin' Technique

"There's not a whole lot to fishing a Carolina rig," Yelas insists. "You don't have to be an accurate caster, and there's nothing special about the retrieve. In fact, there are times when you'll catch more fish by setting the rod down in the boat."

You can use practically any kind of soft-plastic bait. A lizard is a good all-around choice during the pre-spawn period. Bass are active then, so a big bait with good action draws the most strikes. During and after spawning, a smaller, less conspicuous bait, such as a "French fry" or crawworm (below) is a better choice. Normally, the bait is Texas-rigged so it doesn't foul with weeds and debris, but it can be fished with an open hook if the bottom is clean.

Yelas prefers pumpkin and green hues for most of his Carolina rigging. "Haven't been anyplace where I couldn't catch fish on these colors," he said. In clear water, he prefers translucent baits, but if the visibility is less than two feet, he switches to solid-colored baits, usually with a touch of chartreuse.

The taller the vegetation, the longer the leader you'll need. Bass in the weeds are less active than those along the weedline, and they often suspend near the weedtops. Some anglers use a leader up to seven feet in length to keep the bait high enough that the bass can see it.

In very clear water, you'll have better success with lighter line and a lighter sinker. Instead of 20-pound line and a 12-pound leader, use 12-pound line, an 8-pound leader and a lighter rod and reel. Instead of a 1-ounce sinker, try a ¼-ounce. With this lighter gear, the technique is more like split-shotting (p. 20).

Although draggin' works on any structure with a fairly clean bottom, you'll maximize your odds by pinpointing the inside weedline, positioning your boat just outside of it and casting perpendicular to it. If you position the boat too far outside the weedline, you'll encounter dense weeds.

Using a 7-foot, long-handled rod, make a two-hand power cast. The long rod gives you extra distance and makes it easier to wield a long leader. Wait until the rig hits bottom, drag it about 4 to 6 inches with your rod tip, pause, then drag it again. How long you pause depends on the mood of the bass. As a rule, the closer to spawning time, the longer the pause.

Sometimes strikes are aggressive, but more often, you'll just notice a bit more or less weight on the rod tip. Spectra line helps telegraph these subtle takes. When you feel something different, reel up slack until you feel the rod "load," and set the hook. The high-speed reel makes it easier to take up the slack, and the long rod and low-stretch line give you a stronger hook set.

There is no need to horse the fish in open cover. Take your time and let the fish play itself out before you attempt to land it.

"Not only is Carolina riggin' simple," Yelas concludes, "it's the best way to milk a school of bass, because you catch both aggressive and inactive fish. What other technique will do that?"

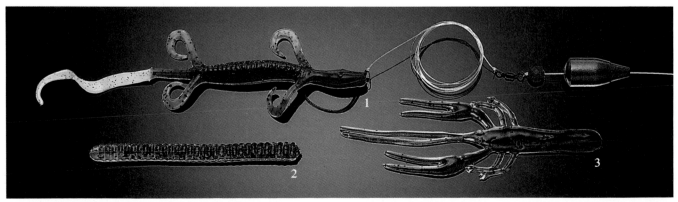

MAKE a Carolina rig by sliding a 1-ounce bullet sinker and a glass bead onto 20-pound mono or 30-pound Spectra, tying on a size 10 barrel swivel, then adding a 3-foot, 12-pound mono leader. Attach a 3/0 HP hook for a (1) lizard; 2/0 for a (2) French fry or (3) crawworm. The glass bead keeps the sinker from damaging the knot, and makes a clicking sound. The lighter leader prevents losing the entire rig should the hook get snagged.

CUSTOM-COLOR soft-plastic baits by dipping them in a specially formulated dye, such as Dip-n-Glo.

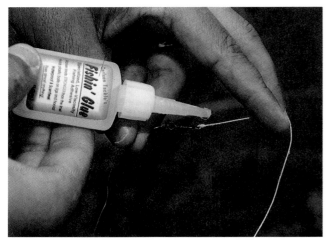

SECURE knots in Spectra or other braided line using waterproof glue, such as Fishin' Glue. It will prevent the knot from slipping and the tag end from fraying.

WORK the shady side of isolated bushes between the inside weedline and shore to catch bass that are moving toward their spawning areas.

SHAKE your sinker while moving the rig forward as little as possible. The commotion and silt stirred up by the sinker trigger strikes when fishing is tough.

CHECK your sinker for evidence of bottom composition. If you find mud in the sinker's hole, for instance, the bottom is probably too soft. Bass prefer a sandy bottom.

Split-Shotting Finicky Largemouth

Optimal Conditions:

Type of Water: deep, clear lakes with sparse cover

Season: spring, summer, fall

Water Temperature: above 55°F

Weather: best under less-than-ideal conditions, such as sunny skies and cold fronts

Water Stage: normal, stable

Water Depth: less than 20 feet

Water Clarity: moderately clear to very clear

Time of Day: anytime

Writers have dreamt up numerous ways to describe finicky bass. They're in a "negative feeding mode," they've got "lockjaw," they're on a "pressure bite," they've got the "post-spawn blues," etc., etc.

Mike Folkestad, well-known touring pro from Yorba Linda, California, has heard all of these terms and has coined a few of his own. That's because he regularly fishes on clear western reservoirs, where bass are notoriously hard to catch. Their finicky habits result from heavy fishing pressure combined with very clear water, which allows them to closely scrutinize their food.

After trying every conceivable method to tempt these fussy biters, Folkestad, like many other bass pros around the country who have been faced with similar conditions, has come to rely heavily on "split-shotting." A form of "finesse fishing," the technique involves small, natural-looking baits fished very slowly on a split-shot rig with light line. "I've known about split-shotting for more than 20 years," Folkestad said. "The fish in this clear water are real sight- oriented.

Day in and day out, you'll get more bites on lighter line and smaller baits – it's a proven fact."

In areas that have been heavily fished by other anglers, split-shotting is an excellent "cleanup" technique. Even wary fish that have been bombarded by big baits for days may grab a small soft-plastic bait presented very slowly.

Mike Folkestad

Hometown:
Yorba Linda, California

Favorite Waters for Technique:
Castaic, Hodges and San Vicente lakes, California; Lake Lanier, Georgia; Harris chain, Florida

Career Highlights:
Winner: 1985 U.S. Open; 1992 Florida BASSMASTER Invitational; 1994 WON BASS Western Classic1990-91 WON BASS Southern Angler of the Year

Split-shotting works best on a rock pile or other structure on the structure

When and Where to Try Split-Shotting

"When you're split-shotting, look for the structure on the structure," Folkestad advises. This is a slow, precise technique that does not cover much water, so you must pick out a likely holding area and work it thoroughly.

During the pre-spawn period, for instance, bass congregate on long, slowly tapering points that top out at about 15 feet, with deep water around them. Using a graph, look for a rock pile, large boulder, clump of brush, a finger projecting off to the side, or anything different that might draw bass. The best points often dip a little at the end, then come back up again before dropping into deep water.

A graph can also help you find what Folkestad refers to as "the activity zone," the layer of water where most fish and baitfish are spotted. Folkestad prefers to fish structure in this zone.

Clear water is best for this technique; in low-clarity water, the fish may not notice such small baits. Split-shotting is easiest in water no deeper than 20 feet. With a rig this light, it would be difficult to fish in deeper water and to maintain good "feel." Because of the light line and the separation between the weight and lure, the rig is not well suited for use in brush or other heavy cover.

Split-shotting is effective any time of day and in all but the coldest months of the year. At water temperatures below 55°F, the bass go deep and are more easily caught by vertically jigging. Another good cold-water technique is to "doodle" a Texas-rigged plastic worm by shaking it as it sinks and after it reaches bottom.

The mood of the bass also helps determine whether or not to use the split-shotting technique. It's a good choice after a cold front, whenever fishing pressure or boating activity is heavy, under sunny skies, at spawning time or anytime the bass are fussy. It may not be the best choice when the bass are actively feeding. Then, they're more likely to strike larger, faster-moving baits, which also improve your odds for big bass.

Split-Shotting Techniques

Equipment:
Rod: 7-foot, medium-power, high-sensitivity graphite spinning rod
Reel: spinning reel with smooth drag
Line: 6- to 8-pound, low-visibility, soft mono
Bait: small plastic grubs, worms and eels

What makes split-shotting so effective under adverse conditions is the bait's lazy action. A Texas-rigged bait sinks rapidly because the weight stays with it. But a bait on a split-shot rig sinks much more slowly, because the weight is separate. The slow sink rate is the key to tempting finicky bass.

Always use round split shot; the winged type tend to catch on bottom and ruin your feel. Select the lightest shot that will still allow you to maintain bottom contact. When the wind is buffeting your line, replace the split shot with a bullet sinker, and secure it on the line with strands of live rubber (p. 93). In brushy cover, a cylindrical weight (p. 24) is the best choice.

Hook selection is also important. An ordinary worm hook is too heavy, so the bait will sink too fast. A fine-wire hook slows the sink rate, giving the fish extra time to examine and grab the bait. And this type of hook penetrates more easily, an important consideration when using light line.

The distance between the hook and shot makes a difference too. Where the cover is sparse, a spread of about 15 inches is ideal. But in weeds, the spread must be greater, as much as 36 inches, so the bait stays above the cover, where bass can see it.

The technique is simple, but your presentation must be very precise in terms of location, speed and depth. Once you find the structure on the structure, make a long cast and feed line until the rig hits bottom. The longer-than-normal rod and light line help in casting the lightweight rig. Light line also makes it easier to feel bottom and detect subtle pickups.

Keeping your rod tip low, inch the bait in slowly by "stitching" line (p. 24), maintaining bottom contact at all times. When it reaches a likely spot, slow down even more to tempt any bass that are there.

Concentrate intently; if you detect any bump or hesitation, or the bait just gets heavier, set the hook. With the sharp, fine-wire hook, there is no need for a powerful hook set that could snap the light line.

"Split-shotting may not be the best way to catch big bass," Folkestad explained, "but it's a great tournament technique because it's so consistent. You can catch a limit, then scale up (switch to larger baits) and go back to get some bigger ones."

How to Rig Popular Split-shotting Baits

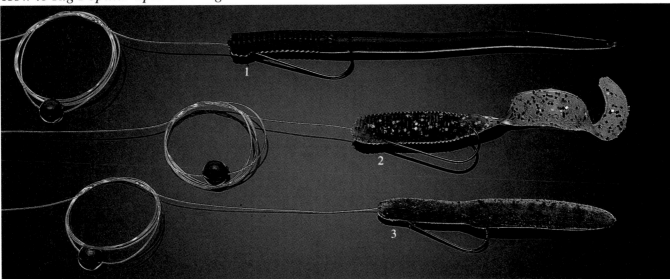

RIG a (1) 4-inch worm, such as a Berkley Finesse Power Worm, using a size 1 hook. This bait works well in cool water (early spring/late fall) because it has minimal action. Rig a (2) 4-inch curlytail, such as a Yamamoto Grub, the same way. This bait is a better choice in warm water because of the rapid tail movement. Rig a (3) 2½-inch eel, such as a Reaper, flat side up with a size 2 hook. This bait is a good choice, spring through fall. Skin-hook the baits as shown for easier hook sets. Natural colors, such as shad, bluegill and crawfish hues, work best.

How to Fish a Split-shot Rig

POSITION your boat upwind of the structure you want to fish (dotted line), then use your troll motor to hold the boat within casting distance. This way, you can use the wind to your advantage for longer casts, and the wind won't bow your line. In very windy weather, you may have to anchor to maintain good feel.

HOLD your rod low and pointed toward the bait, so wind won't catch your line. When you feel the bait bumping cover, slow down; inch it in with no jumps or twitches.

SET the hook anytime you feel spongy resistance; a lethargic bass may just pick up the bait and hold it. Set with a firm sideways sweep.

Split-shotting Tips

BORE a cavity in a grub using a Grub-Gutter. Insert the hook point in the cavity for easier penetration, or put a float or rattle in the cavity.

SUBSTITUTE a cylindrical weight, such as a Mojo sinker, for a split shot. The slender sinker slips through brush more easily.

STITCH in line with your fingers to detect bottom changes and subtle bites. When a few feet of slack accumulates, reel it up and stitch some more.

24

Hook a crayfish through the bony horn with a small, short-shank hook, size 4 or 6

The Crayfish Option

When fishing is really tough, even "finesse baits" may fail to draw a strike, but bass will seldom refuse a live, 2½- to 4-inch crayfish. And crayfish account for more trophy largemouth, wary fish that usually ignore artificials.

Folkestad prefers to hook the crayfish through the horn (above), with a split shot for weight, or no weight at all. This way, he can pull it ahead a short distance, let it scoot backwards, then pull it ahead again, making for a very natural presentation.

There are times when bass will eat any crayfish, hardshell or softshell, small or large. But when the fish are superfussy, it's important to select the smaller, softer-shelled crayfish.

You can also make a large crayfish appear smaller and less formidable by removing one or both claws. To remove a claw, squeeze it with your fingers and it will detach from the body neatly. If you rip the claw off, you may kill the crayfish.

Crayfish must be worked very slowly, so the best method is to anchor the boat near a likely spot and cast. Anchor from both the bow and stern so the boat can't move. Lob the crayfish out so it doesn't tear off the hook, then feed line until it reaches bottom.

The retrieve is excruciatingly slow, sometimes taking as long as 5 minutes. When you feel a pickup, reel up the slack until you feel slight tension, then set the hook. A bass usually inhales the crayfish, so if you wait too long to set, you may hook the fish so deeply it won't survive.

Soft Stickbaits:
Breakthrough for Stubborn Bass

At first glance, a soft stickbait is not much to get excited about. The plastic is harder and stiffer than most other soft-plastic baits, and it has no legs, tentacles or curly tail to give it action, so its appearance is certainly not lifelike. But many would argue that this bait is the most significant bass-fishing innovation in recent years.

David Vance, one of East Texas' best-known guides and a regular on the BASSMASTER tournament trail, is one such soft-stickbait proponent. "Its near-neutral buoyancy and enticing, dying-baitfish action work magic on big bass," he maintains, "even when they have the post-spawn blues."

Vance does most of his fishing on Lake Fork, the state's premier trophy bass factory, which produces astounding numbers of 10- to 18-pound "sows." He knows the best time to catch the giant bass is around the spawning period, but he also knows just how finicky they can be at that time.

"They turn up their noses at fast-moving baits," Vance says. "But you can put this bait right in their face and tease them into hitting it. And once they grab it, they won't let go."

Optimal Conditions:
Type of Water: any lake or river with clarity of at least 1 foot
Season: spawn through post-spawn
Water Temperature: 55 to 70°F.
Weather: calm, overcast
Water Stage: stable or slowly rising
Water Depth: 10 feet or less
Time of Day: all day if skies are overcast; otherwise, early and late in day

The major drawback to these baits is the difficulty of fishing them in windy weather. They can be a problem to cast, and when the wind catches your line, it pulls the bait through the water too fast. Because these baits must be fished so slowly at this time of year, they're not a good choice for covering lots of water.

The original soft stickbait, the Slug-Go, was introduced in 1990, and within a few years, its popularity swept the country. Today, fishermen can choose from dozens of different soft-stickbait brands.

David Vance

Hometown:
Winnsboro, Texas
Favorite Waters for Technique:
Lakes Fork, Sam Rayburn, Toledo Bend, all in Texas
Career Highlights:
Well-known guide on Lake Fork; 36 ten-pound-plus bass; 2nd place – 1991 Texas BASS-MASTER BP Top 100

WORK any visible spawning beds in shallow, sandy areas to catch nest-guarding males; work the areas between the beds for cruising bass. Your chances of catching the larger females are better around woody cover just outside the bedding area; females stage there before and after spawning.

When and Where to Try Soft-Stickin'

Soft-stickin' excels once bass move onto the spawning grounds. They're much less aggressive than they were in the pre-spawn period, and they stay that way until late in the post-spawn. The bait's slow sink rate is a plus this time of year because the fish are in shallow water, usually less than 10 feet. Once they move deeper, however, soft-stickin' becomes less effective.

Concentrate on the creek arms where bass are known to spawn. The best ones tend to be long and narrow, so the spawning beds are protected from the wind.

They have only small creeks feeding them, so they stay fairly clear. Avoid fishing creek arms with muddy water.

A soft stickbait produces practically no sound or vibration, so the water must be clear enough for bass to see it. As a rule, use soft stickbaits only when the visibility is a foot or more.

Soft-stickin' works best under low-light conditions – early or late in the day or under cloudy skies. Under high sun, the bass stick tight to the cover, where they're less aggressive and more difficult to reach with a soft stickbait, which won't penetrate the cover as well as a jig or Texas-rigged worm. Evenings are usually better than mornings, because warming water makes the fish more aggressive.

The Lone-Star Lunker Program

The chances of catching a 10-pound Texas largemouth have skyrocketed in recent years, thanks in part to the "Operation Share a Lone-Star Lunker Program," or "LSL." This coop venture between the Texas Parks and Wildlife Department, various corporate sponsors and anglers, provides TPWD with wild brood stock bass used to improve their propagation program.

Anglers who turn in a bass weighing 13 pounds or more to TPWD are given a fiberglass replica of their fish, courtesy of the corporate sponsors. Taking eggs from large, wild bass not only selects for large size, it increases genetic variability. If only captive brood stock are used, inbreeding can be a serious problem. Using wild brood stock also increases the chances that the offspring will spawn in the wild. And the fact that the parent was caught on hook and line increases the likelihood that the offspring will be catchable.

To date, more than 125 lunkers have been turned in by anglers, including a former state-record 17.65-pounder, and the present state record, an 18.18-pounder (right). Although a relatively small percentage of these fish have spawned in captivity, TPWD officials are confident that new facilities and techniques will improve spawning success. A new hatchery recently opened to care for these lunkers and to better duplicate natural conditions by precisely controlling water temperature and photoperiod.

Once TPWD is finished with the fish, they are returned alive to the anglers who caught them. Most are then released back into the waters from which they came. Several of the fish have been caught again, and one fish was entered in the program a second time.

Not only has the LSL program created a positive relationship between anglers and fisheries managers, it has boosted public awareness of the importance of catch and release of largemouth bass. The program has also taught many fishermen how to properly handle big bass; tournament and recreational anglers are successfully releasing more bass than ever before.

Texas angler Barry St. Clair donating his 18.18-pound Texas-record bass to LSL

Slot Limits: The Perfect Fishing Regulations?

Slot limits protect a given-size class of fish. On Lake Fork, for instance, a slot limit of 14 to 21 inches was established in 1989. This means you can keep bass under 14 inches and over 21, but those in between must be returned to the water. In 1993, the regulation was altered slightly to allow only one bass over 21 inches.

A study conducted by the Texas Parks and Wildlife Department showed that the number of bass over 18 inches long more than tripled from 1988, before the regulation was imposed, to 1993.

Of all possible types of size regulations, slot limits make the most biological sense for protecting waters with good fish populations. Other regulations, such as minimum size limits, may work better when fish populations are low. Here's why slot limits are so effective:

• They protect the prime spawning stock, fish that have just reached sexual maturity. The large, old fish that most people assume are the prime spawners may be well past their spawning peak, and their eggs often have a very low hatch rate.

• They ensure a continuing supply of fish that will grow to trophy size in the next few years. If anglers harvest the small fish, as the regulations allow, competition among fish in that size class is reduced, resulting in faster growth of those that remain.

• The width of the slot can be adjusted to suit existing fish populations. It can be widened when populations are low, narrowed when they're high and moved up or down to allow harvest of strong-year classes.

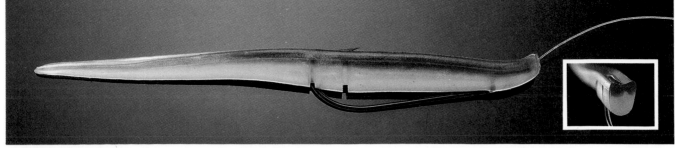

RIG a stickbait, such as a Lunker City Slug-Go, so it rides straight, with head angled upward (opposite). The lighter the cover, the more you can push the hook point through the plastic without risk of fouling. The point is protected by the bait's concave back (inset of cross-section) or, in some brands, a slot.

The Soft-Stickin' Technique

The secret to catching bass on a soft stickbait is to keep your presentation slow. Just cast the bait and retrieve it with short twitches followed by pauses, varying the cadence until you find the right combination. The bait should dart randomly with each rod twitch, rather than veer from side to side in a predictable fashion. Between twitches, it will suspend momentarily, then slowly sink.

The bait is rigged with a long-shank offset hook, which keeps the center of gravity toward the middle of the bait and ensures that it sinks in a horizontal position. With a shorter-shank hook, the bait would nosedive and sink much faster. Heavy line, 15- to 20-pound mono, helps keep the nose up.

When rigged properly, the bait should have a slight upward bend at the head (opposite). This way, the bait will plane upward when you twitch it, then glide back down.

Vance normally favors a natural greenish shiner color, but he uses darker colors in muddy water or on cloudy days. In clearer-than-normal water, he often switches to a blue-back shiner color.

Soft stickbaits may be difficult to cast. If you cast into the wind, for instance, they slow down quickly and you end up with a backlash. Try to cast straight downwind and keep your rod tip low when retrieving to minimize the bow the wind puts in your line.

Bass usually grab the bait on the pause, as it settles. You may feel a tap, see the line jump or move off to the side, or just feel extra resistance. Then, quickly reel up all your slack and set the hook with a hard wrist snap. A beefy rod is a must to drive the big hook into the jaw, and to horse a fish from the cover once it's hooked.

"You got to be on your toes at all times when you're soft-stickin'," Vance explains. "If you're not paying attention, a bass may grab the bait and you won't even know it. But once you learn the system, you'll catch more big fish than you ever dreamed about."

Soft-stickbait Tips

STORE soft stickbaits so they stay straight by laying them one by one in long-enough compartments. If they warp, they won't dart randomly.

PUSH a lead insert or nail into the bait just ahead of the hook bend. The bait will cast better and run deeper, and the wind won't move it as fast.

How to Fish a Soft Stickbait

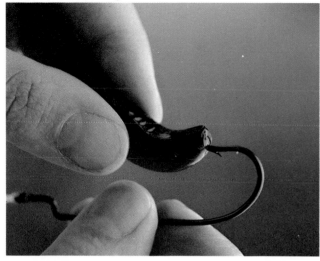

1. INSERT the hook as shown so the head of the bait has a slight upward bend.

2. TWITCH the bait, with your rod angled downward, to make it dart.

3. PAUSE to let the bait glide on a slack line; finicky bass like long pauses.

4. SET the hook sharply so the thick hook will penetrate the bass's jaw.

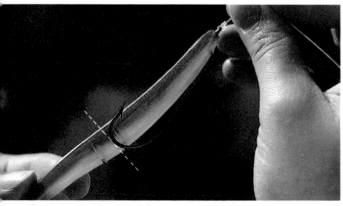

LAY the hook over the bait and draw an imaginary line at the rear of the bend. Push the hook through the body along this line to ensure that the bait rides straight.

BOIL warped baits for about 30 seconds. Lay them on their back to dry, making sure they're straight. Boiling them too long softens them too much.

Advanced Jigging Techniques

Yo-Yoing for Bass in Dense Milfoil

Optimal Conditions:

Type of Water: any lake with deep milfoil beds
Season: post-spawn through early fall
Water Temperature: upper 60s or higher
Weather: calm, sunny
Water Stage: normal, stable
Water Depth: 15 feet or less
Water Clarity: 2 feet or more
Time of Day: late morning to early evening

Eurasian water milfoil – the very mention of it causes panic among boaters and lakeshore property owners. As its name suggests, this fast-growing aquatic plant is native to Europe and Asia, as well as northern Africa. It was found in the Chesapeake Bay area in the late 1800s, and since that time has spread to 37 states and 3 Canadian provinces.

The plant infests natural and man-made lakes, growing to depths of 15 feet or more and forming a dense canopy at the surface or several feet below it. The matted plants interfere with boating and crowd out other aquatic plants. And fragments of them wash in and foul the beaches.

For bass and bass fishermen, however, not all the news about milfoil is bad. "The thick canopy provides shade, security and cooler temperatures for largemouth," explained Pat Martin, a successful tournament angler who spends a lot of his time fishing Minnesota's Lake Minnetonka, a 14,000-acre natural lake infested with Eurasian water milfoil. "There's been a big increase in the number and size of the bass since the milfoil explosion." Many other natural and man-made lakes around the country also underwent a bass boom soon after milfoil was established. "But milfoil is tough to fish," Martin says. "With so much of it, most fishermen don't know where to find the

bass. And even if they can find them, they have trouble getting a lure to them."

With the rapid spread of Eurasian water milfoil, anglers coast-to-coast are having the same problems. The bass may not be in the traditional spots, and the old techniques may no longer be as effective. But by understanding the locational patterns and using the angling techniques that follow, you'll catch more bass than ever.

These techniques will work on any milfoil-ridden natural lake with clear water, but they can also be used on man-made lakes and on lakes overrun with other dense weeds, such as hydrilla.

Pat Martin

Hometown:
Chanhassen, Minnesota
Favorite Waters for Technique:
Lake Minnetonka and Clearwater Lake, Minnesota
Career Highlights:
1991 Minnesota Team of the Year on both the American Scholarship and Minnesota/Wisconsin Pro-Am circuits
Winner of 6 tournaments on the same circuits

Midsummer milfoil canopy provides ideal cover for largemouth bass

Sprig of Eurasian water milfoil, and leaflets of Eurasian (top inset) and northern (bottom) inset) water milfoil

Understanding Milfoil

Eurasian water milfoil is easily confused with several native North American milfoil species. But it can usually be distinguished by its finer, more closely spaced leaflets. While native milfoil species seldom grow in water deeper than 10 feet, Eurasian milfoil thrives in water as deep as 30, so it covers a much greater portion of a lake bed.

Considered one of the most aggressive and troublesome of all aquatic plants, Eurasian milfoil may interfere with swimming and boating, detract from a lake's aesthetic appeal, clog water intakes, interfere with fish spawning, lower oxygen content of the water and even increase mosquito populations. But despite all these adverse impacts, many milfoil-infested lakes are producing more and bigger bass than ever. A number of old reservoirs, where the woody cover has deteriorated, have been rejuvenated by establishment of milfoil.

Milfoil provides hiding cover for small bass and ambush cover for big ones. And the dense vegetation makes an ideal surface for aquatic invertebrates, an important link in the aquatic food chain.

The plant flourishes in a wide variety of lakes, but reaches its highest density in those with fine-textured, inorganic sediments. It is not as abundant in highly fertile lakes with turbid water and an organic ooze bottom, or in deep, infertile lakes.

Eurasian milfoil grows rapidly in spring, beginning when the water temperature reaches the upper 50s. There may be a second growth spurt in late summer. When the shoots reach the surface, they branch profusely and flower, forming heavy mats in the shallows. Even before the mats form, the dense growth prevents the lower leaves from getting enough sunlight, so they begin to drop off. By midsummer, the mats remain, with surprisingly little vegetation below.

In deep lakes, the milfoil canopy may be several feet beneath the surface, and dense surface mats form only near shore. The tendency of the plant to mat in shallow water means that the densest growth takes place in low-water years.

Wind and currents move leaf fragments from one part of a lake to another, where it quickly reroots. Outboard motors also rip up milfoil beds, producing fragments that are likely to spread. Milfoil fragments are transported from one body of water to another via boat trailers and water birds.

Once Eurasian milfoil gains a foothold in a lake, it soon overwhelms other native aquatic plants, sometimes crowding them out completely. The milfoil generally maintains its dominance for 5 to 10 years, then gradually declines in density.

Attempts to eradicate or control the spread of Eurasian milfoil have been only minimally successful. Chemical treatments have never shown long-term results, although growth can be controlled with regular applications. Methods such as harvesting, dredging and derooting may actually promote milfoil growth. In some lakes, milfoil growth has continued unabated in disturbed areas but declined in undisturbed areas. In British Columbia, the spread of milfoil from lake to lake was slowed only slightly by a major public education and road-check program.

Research is currently underway to test "selective" chemicals, those that kill only certain plants, including milfoil. But even if such treatments prove successful, they would be too expensive for wide-scale use. Other possible control measures include introduction of a variety of insects that damage milfoil. There is evidence to suggest that some natural declines have been insect-related.

When and Where to Find Milfoil Bass

Bass use milfoil throughout the year. They often spawn along the inside edges of shallow milfoil beds at depths of 1 to 4 feet, either in sheltered bays or along protected shorelines. After spawning, when the males have abandoned the fry, you'll find bass on milfoil flats adjacent to spawning areas. Look for dense clumps of milfoil that grow nearly to the surface, usually in water from 8 to 12 feet deep.

"Let's say you're fishing a flat with a blanket of milfoil 4 feet beneath the surface," Martin proposed. "Then you come across a small area with milfoil 1 to 2 feet under the surface – that's where you want to fish in the post-spawn."

Often, these milfoil clumps are found on a slight rise, but they may also grow where the bottom is perfectly flat. On a calm, sunny day, the clumps are easy to spot. Those with schools of sunfish in or around them are the most likely to hold bass.

The depth at which you find post-spawn bass depends on their activity level. As a rule, the more active they are, the higher they'll be in the milfoil. Feeding bass cruise just beneath the milfoil canopy or even on top of it; bass in a neutral or negative mood stay near the bottom and move very little.

As summer progresses, largemouth move closer to the break at the outer edge of a milfoil bed, usually holding in 10 to 15 feet of water. There, the sharp drop-off gives them easy access to deeper water.

Bare spots on points or inside turns, or anywhere along the weedline, are the hub of summertime bass activity. These bare spots, most of which are less than 20 feet in diameter, are simply hard-bottomed areas where milfoil can't take root.

When bass are most active, usually during low-light conditions, they move about and feed right on the bare spots. When they're less active, as is often the case on sunny days, they tuck into thick weed clumps near the bare spots and move about much less.

Bass using these bare spots in summer provide the year's best and most consistent fishing. A school of bass may hold on the same spot for weeks at a time. They remain in these locations until the milfoil begins to turn brown in late summer or early fall. Then the consistency of the pattern breaks down; the fish begin to move about more and spend more of their time feeding in shallower water.

By fall turnover, most of the bass have abandoned the deep bare spots. You'll find them relating to shallower bare spots or areas of sparse milfoil growth, usually from 5 to 8 feet deep but sometimes as shallow as 3. Check bare spots within milfoil beds or along their sandy inside edges. Don't overlook such weed-free areas as boat channels or rock piles within a milfoil bed.

This locational pattern grows even stronger as the water drops below 50°F. Late-season fishing is best when a few warmer-than-normal days stabilize the water temperature. Bass remain in these areas until freeze-up.

How Milfoil Growth Affects Seasonal Bass Location

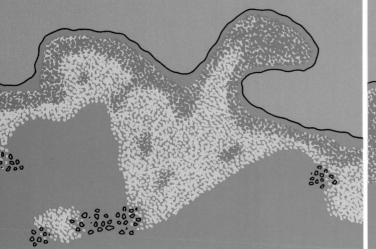 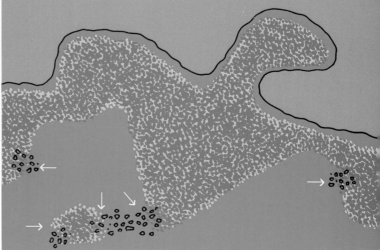

LATE SPRING/EARLY SUMMER. Milfoil growth is heaviest near shore and on shallow humps, with only a few scattered clumps of tall milfoil in deeper water on adjacent flats. Bass relate to the densest milfoil clumps.

MIDSUMMER. Heavy milfoil growth covers the shallows and extends onto deep flats. Only small holes separate the tall milfoil clumps. Look for bass in holes and bare spots (arrows) around the outer edge of the milfoil.

POPULAR LURES for milfoil fishing include (1) Texas-rigged worm, such as a Berkley Power Worm, with a 5/16- to 5/8-ounce bullet sinker and a heavy size 3/0 worm hook;

5/8- to 1-ounce, weedless, bullet-head jig, such as a J-Mac, tipped with (2) Gene Larew Electric Salt Craw or (3) Berkley Power Grub.

How to Yo-Yo the Milfoil

Equipment:

Rod: 6½- to 7- foot, long-handled, medium-heavy-power, fast-action, graphite baitcaster
Reel: baitcasting reel with gear ratio of at least 6:1
Line: 25-pound, low-vis green mono (not low-stretch)
Lure: 5/8- to 1-ounce, weedless bullet-head jig with plastic or pork trailer; Texas-rigged plastic worm

Most anglers detest fishing in milfoil because it's nearly impossible to pull a lure through it without fouling. And if you do hook a fish when casting, it will almost surely tangle in the weeds and escape.

Martin helped develop a unique technique which solves the problem. Called yo-yoing, it involves jigging vertically in the milfoil, using a stiff rod and high-speed reel to horse the fish to the surface before it can tangle.

The best jigs for yo-yoing have a bullet-shaped head with the attachment eye at the tip to minimize fouling, and a large, strong hook that will improve your hooking percentage but won't bend when you hoist in the fish. Use the lightest jig practical for the conditions and a bulky trailer that will slow the sink rate. Dark colors or those that match common foods, such as crayfish, perch or bluegills, work best.

Head with eye at tip (left) is better than one with eye at top (right)

If jigs aren't working, try Texas-rigged plastic worms, and fish them the same way.

To locate bass, start at the downwind edge of the cover and move slowly into the wind. Then, flip the jig into an opening in the milfoil, from a few inches to a few feet in diameter. To keep your line as vertical as possible while you're moving forward, flip into openings slightly ahead of the boat.

Flip just ahead of moving boat

Always fish close to the boat, little more than a rod length away. This way, you can easily feed line and jiggle your rod tip to make the jig sink through the weedy tangle, and you can horse a hooked fish straight up, so it won't wrap in the weeds.

When the jig hits bottom, experiment with different jigging tempos until you find the pattern that works best. The more active the bass, the faster the tempo. When the bass are fussy, try "dead-sticking" them, letting the jig lie motionless for several seconds between each lift. Keep flippin' into different openings as you work into the wind.

38

Rod should be low when jig touches bottom, ready for hook set

With two anglers in the boat, both should stand on the front deck and work water ahead of the boat. If one stands in the back, he will be working water that the boat has already passed over. But an angler in the back of the boat may want to try casting spinnerbaits or crankbaits to pick up any fish cruising high in the milfoil.

Active bass usually inhale the jig on the drop, so you'll feel a tap or notice the jig stop sinking. But when the bass are finicky, they'll just pick up the jig off the bottom, and all you'll feel is a little extra weight. Set the hook hard and crank the fish out of the cover as quickly as possible. If you give the fish a chance to swim around the weeds, it may escape by tangling your line or spook other fish in the school by tearing up the weeds. If you don't hook the fish, flip the jig into the same spot, and try to coax another strike.

Place one hand a foot up the rod for extra hoisting leverage

"Sometimes you have to catch one bass to trigger others in a school to start feeding," said Martin. "It's not unusual to see a school follow a hooked bass to the surface in a wild frenzy."

If this happens, drop your jig back into the same hole, let it fall to bottom, then bring it up and work it just beneath the canopy, where the active bass are most likely to be. You may want to switch to a lighter jig, about 1/2-ounce, that will sink through the upper zone more slowly.

Once activated, some bass in the school begin feeding above the canopy. In this case, you may have better success by fan-casting the area with a spinnerbait, vibrating plug, minnow plug or shallow-running crankbait. Plugs with internal rattles work best; bass can home in on them more easily, so you get more strikes and better hookups.

You'll catch many more bass if you're careful not to spook the school. Put the fish you catch in your live well until you're done fishing a spot. A fish you release or one that breaks your line may alarm the school, and they'll quit biting. Working into the wind also reduces spooking; when you hook a fish, the boat will blow away from the school, not over it.

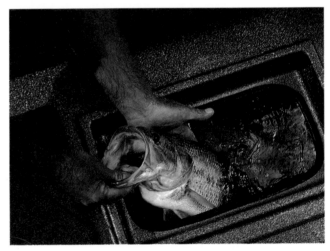

Temporarily store the fish in your live well

When you find a school of bass, note the precise location, toss out a marker and keep working it until the action stops. Then, you may want to switch to a jig of a different size or color, or to a Texas-rigged plastic worm. The change may trigger a few more fish to bite.

Leave your marker in place when you're done working the school, then come back and try the spot again later; there may be a few rocks, taller milfoil, a deeper slot or some other structural element that will draw bass back to the same spot.

High winds make it difficult to jig openings in the submerged milfoil. Not only will you have trouble seeing them, it's difficult to keep your boat in the right position. The wind also buffets your rod tip and deadens your feel, making it necessary to use a jig weighing at least 1 ounce.

BEND the hook shank as shown so the point has a better angle to penetrate a fish's jaw. Touch up the point with a file or hone.

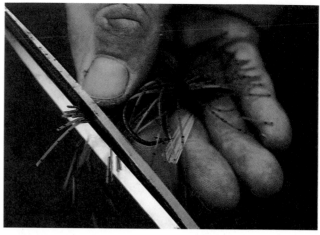

TRIM the rear of the skirt so it is even with the hook bend; trim the front so the strands stand out to form a collar whose fibers will quiver even when the jig is at rest.

SHORTEN the weedguard as shown to improve hooking; the long bristles cover the hook. The tip of the trimmed bristles should stop just short of the hook point.

PUSH the hook into a fat-bodied grub so it rests just under the skin (dotted line). This way, the hook gap stays open, improving your hooking percentage.

SHAKE the jig, then let it rest, to trigger a strike. Sometimes the frantic action draws the attention of bass that ignore an ordinary lift-and-drop presentation.

SECURE a worm with pieces of stiff mono tied to the hook eye. When the worm is pushed over the eye (dotted line), the tag ends prevent it from slipping back.

Work matted milfoil with a surface lure, such as a weedless spoon, on a warm day

Other Milfoil Techniques

After a few warm days in spring, when pre-spawn bass are holding in shallow water along the inner edges of milfoil beds, they'll hit practically anything you throw at them. It pays to use lures that cover a lot of water. Buzzbaits and spinnerbaits are ideal for working pockets in the milfoil and paralleling the edge. When the bass are not as aggressive, try a slower presentation, such as twitching a soft stickbait (p. 30).

In summer and early fall, bass cruise the outer edges of milfoil beds when they're active, and they tuck back into the milfoil when they're not. When they're along the edges, you can catch them on a variety of baits, including medium- to deep-running crank-

Try paralleling the inside weedline with a buzzbait

baits, ribbontail worms on mushroom-head jigs, deep-running spinnerbaits, and the same bullet-head jigs discussed earlier. It's possible to use baits with open hooks, because milfoil growth along the edges is sparse enough that fouling is not a big problem. Try to hold your boat right over the drop-off and cast parallel to the break.

Another good summertime pattern is fishing surface clumps of matted milfoil. Work edges and holes in the clumps with buzzbaits and spinnerbaits; the clumps, themselves, with weedless spoons and hollow-bodied rats and frogs.

When bass move onto shallow milfoil flats in midfall, try slow-rolling a tandem-blade spinnerbait so it just bumps the weedtops, letting it helicopter into openings and slots. Or slowly retrieve a high-buoyancy, shallow- to medium-running crankbait over openings and along shallow edges of the flats. A buoyant plug is more likely to float off of the weeds should it foul. If you feel resistance, set the hook. A strike doesn't feel much different than hooking a milfoil stem. This technique produces fewer but bigger bass than you'd normally catch in summer.

"We're still discovering new ways to fish the milfoil," Martin explained. "When you get milfoil in a lake, it's literally a whole new environment for the fish, and you have to modify your techniques to stay competitive."

Football Jigs:
Magic for Pre-Spawn Bass

When pre-spawn largemouth congregate along steep bluffs before moving into their spawning areas, they can be tough to catch. They're still in deep water and not very aggressive, and the sharp-breaking structure makes fishing a real challenge.

But Ted Miller, winner of the Arizona BASSMASTER Invitational on Lake Havasu in 1989, has devised an unusual technique that triggers these uninterested bass to strike. He's been onto the method for years but, until now, hasn't been doing much talking.

"There are times when this method stands head-and-shoulders above any other," Miller maintains. "In a spring Redman tournament on Lake Havasu, my draw-partner and I both used the technique. We finished one-two."

Miller has now retired from tournament competition, explaining why he agreed to reveal the details of the jigging technique that accounted for much of his tournament success.

Unlike the methods used by most tournament anglers, Miller's technique excels when the fish are holding on steep structure, particularly during the pre-spawn period. But the technique also works well when bass move to steep structure in late fall. The heavy jig with its unusual football-shaped head clinks against rocks and darts rapidly as it bounces down a steep bank, and the bulky, wriggling "spider-jig" body moves a lot of water.

The heavy football jig head enables you to stay in contact with the bottom – a near impossibility on the

Optimal Conditions:

Type of Water: deep, clear, rocky reservoirs with steep structure
Season: pre-spawn, late fall
Water Temperature: 50 to 60°F
Weather: cold, windy, rainy is best
Water Stage: any stage; falling is best
Water Depth: 10 to 35 feet
Water Clarity: moderately clear to very clear
Time of Day: early morning, late afternoon best

steep structure if you use a lighter jig head or one with the attachment eye near the nose. The quick-sinking action is opposite to that recommended by most pros, but is remindful of the darting movements of crayfish, which abound on the steep, rocky structure. Miller believes the wild action triggers "reflex" strikes from bass that are attempting to pick off crayfish before they zip under a rock.

The football head has some other advantages. Its shape keeps the jig head and hook riding upright, and when the jig is worked slowly over a gravelly bottom, the head pivots each time it bumps into a pebble, making the body move up and down and creating an enticing action.

Although the technique evolved on western reservoirs, it will work wherever the bass are holding in deep, clear water and feeding on crayfish.

Ted Miller

Hometown:
Apache Junction, Arizona
Favorite Waters for Technique:
Colorado River reservoirs
Career Highlights:
Winner: 1987 U.S. Bass World Championship; 1989 Arizona BASSMASTER Invitational; 1989 Lake Mead Golden Blend Diamond Invitational; Three-time qualifier, Red Man All-American

Where and When to Find Pre-Spawn Bass in Deep Western Reservoirs

The key to finding pre-spawn bass is knowing where to find their spawning areas and concentrating on adjacent deep water. In reservoirs of this type, largemouth spawn in the back ends of coves. Before they spawn, you'll find them along steep bluffs leading into the back ends.

Early in the pre-spawn period, when the water temperature reaches about 50°F, look for bass along bluffs at the junction of a cove and the main lake.

Features that Concentrate Pre-spawn Bass

IRREGULAR POINTS plunging into deep water are best.

SHADED INDENTATIONS hold bass on sunny days.

STEEP BLUFFS lead bass into spawning coves.

As the water warms and spawning time nears, they work their way farther into the cove, hugging the bluff until they're adjacent to the spawning area. They'll stay there until the water temperature reaches the low 60s.

Bass tend to hold near any irregular features along the bluff. Look for rock slides, points, indentations and ledges with some kind of cover, such as a rubble pile or brush clump.

Typical depths during the pre-spawn period are 10 to 35 feet, but the fish can be considerably deeper if the water is extremely clear. The best spots have water much deeper than that in which the bass are holding; this way, the fish can easily retreat to whatever depths they wish.

The spots that draw bass during the pre-spawn period also attract them in fall. But the fall pattern is not as reliable, because the turnover scatters the fish about the lake.

The technique works best in cold, raw weather, as evidenced by an experience Miller had in a bass tournament on Nevada's Lake Mead. "First day, the rain would hit your raincoat and freeze," he recalled. "I caught 16 pounds, next closest guy had 6. Next day, it cleared up and I blanked. Still won the tournament though."

In sunny weather, the fish usually bite best in the morning, before sunlight begins to hit the bluff face. Afterward, look for any shaded indentation.

Water stage is not a major consideration, although the technique tends to be most effective under stable or falling conditions. In rising water, bass move onto shallow flats or into flooded brush where you would probably do better using other methods.

RUBBLE PILES on underwater ledges make ideal cover.

ROCK SLIDES indicate good underwater structure.

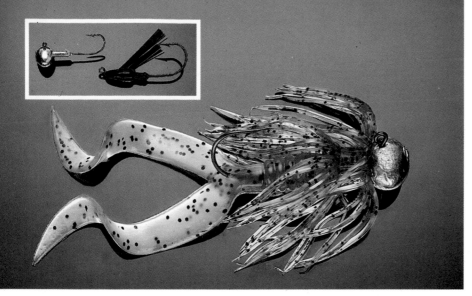

Miller's Football-Jigging Techniques

Equipment:
Rod: 6½-foot heavy-power, fast-action graphite baitcaster
Reel: high-speed baitcaster
Line: 12- to 14-pound mono
Lures: football-head spider jig

Miller's jigging technique involves casting a football-head spider jig (left) toward a steep-breaking bluff or shoreline. He normally uses a ¾-ounce jig head, but for windy weather or deep water, he switches to a 1-ounce. His favorite color is

MILLER'S FAVORITE JIG has a ¾- to 1-ounce football head (contact Jerry's Jigs, Peoria, Arizona or Do-it Molds, Denver, Iowa), a Yamamoto Tease Skirt and a Bass'N Man 4-inch Double-tail. A football head (left in inset) is a better choice than a standard brushguard jig head (right in inset). Because of its more compact shape, vertical attachment eye and fine-wire hook, it sinks more vertically, hugs bottom tighter, has a more enticing, rocking action and hooks fish better.

How to Jig the Bluffs

1. CAST to the base of the bluff wall, quickly lift your rod to spin off extra line, engage the reel and allow the jig to free-fall to the bottom on a semislack line.

2. HOP the jig with a 6- to 12-inch vertical twitch, raising your rod to about 10 o'clock. Then let the jig sink again, feeding more line, if necessary.

3. FOLLOW the jig with your rod tip as it free-falls again. Keep the line taut enough to feel strikes, but not so taut that the jig won't sink vertically. The rod should stop at about 8 o'clock.

4. CRANK-SET the hook by reeling as fast as you can while lifting your rod high. A crank-set takes up the slack created by the rapidly sinking jig. Play the fish with steady pressure, allowing it to tire in deep water.

pumpkin-pepper, because it closely matches the color of a crayfish.

Position your boat within 25 or 30 feet of the bluff and cast perpendicular so your jig lands near the base. If you attempt to fish parallel to the bluff face, as most anglers normally would, you'll be snagged constantly.

The trickiest part of this technique is working your jig precisely the right way. You may have to vary your retrieve, using longer or shorter hops, until you find the action the bass prefer.

This type of jigging is tough on monofilament line, because the heavy jig is constantly dragging the line over rocks. Retie often, and check your line frequently by giving it a sharp tug.

A jig this heavy sinks much faster than the line, so you're always fighting a bow in your line. This may cause a problem when trying to set the hook, unless you use a fine-wire hook, a long, stiff rod and a high-speed reel, and "crankset" the hook (opposite).

Let the fish tire out in deep water, then land it as shown below. The heavy head and fine-wire hook make the jig easy to shake and if you horse the fish, it's more likely to jump and throw the hook.

Nestle the gunwale in your armpit for maximum reach when lip landing

"I'm surprised this technique hasn't really caught on," said Miller. "You can catch a good limit of bass on a blustery day when guys throwing light jigs and crankbaits just give up."

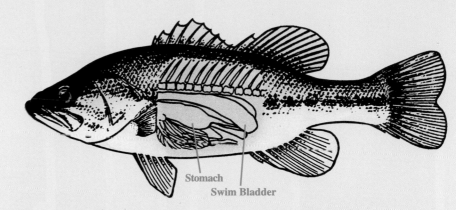

Stomach
Swim Bladder

Position of swim bladder in a largemouth bass

How to De-Gas a Largemouth

When you pull a fish from water deeper than 30 feet, its swim bladder (above) inflates as a result of the reduced water pressure at the surface. Sometimes the swim bladder swells up enough to force the stomach out the mouth. Because of the added buoyancy and exhaustion from the fight, the fish may not be able to descend or right itself, so it flounders upside down on the surface.

These symptoms are seldom seen in *physostomous* fish, such as trout and salmon, because they have a duct connecting the swim bladder and esophagus. They can rapidly eliminate excess gas by "burping" it up, and can easily swim back down when released.

The symptoms are most noticeable in *physoclistous* fish, like largemouth bass, which do not have a duct connecting their swim bladder and esophagus. To eliminate excess gas, they must metabolize it, which can be a slow process, especially when their metabolic rate is low due to cold water. Use the following procedures to successfully release these fish:

Reel the fish in quickly to avoid sapping its strength. If the stomach is not protruding from the mouth,

release the fish immediately. Dropping it nose-first will help give it the momentum it needs to return to the depths, where increased water pressure compresses the swim bladder. If you do not release the fish immediately, gas bubbles will accumulate in the blood, as well, lessening survival chances.

If the fish is not strong enough to overcome the buoyancy of its swim bladder, it will float back to the surface. The body will look swollen, and the stomach may be protruding from the mouth. Retrieve it and de-gas it as shown below.

Remove a scale and insert an 18- or 20-gauge hypodermic needle at the point indicated below, then listen for the escaping gas. You may have to push on the belly to force out the gas. If the stomach does not retract from the mouth, poke it down the throat with a blunt object.

When you release the fish, watch to make sure it doesn't float back up. If it does, de-gas it again, or keep it.

Fish pulled from water more than 50 feet deep may have more serious problems including ruptured blood vessels and gas bubbles in vital organs. If you see blood spots on the body or fins, or bugged-out eyes, the fish will probably die; it makes no sense to throw it back.

Insert needle 3 to 5 scale rows below lateral line, on line between notch in dorsal fins and vent

Jig-Drifting: Natural Approach for River Largemouth

When it comes to locating bass in rivers, current can be your ally or your enemy. If you understand how bass respond to these variables, they become quite predictable, and you can establish a consistent fish-catching pattern. If not, your success will be spotty.

Rich Zaleski, well-known outdoor writer from Stevenson, Connecticut, and past winner of the North American Bass Association Tournament of Champions, has some simple advice for fishing moving water: "Learn where to find the fish at different water stages, and present your bait naturally."

Zaleski relies heavily on jigs for fishing moving water, but he fishes them much differently than in lakes. "The jig should be buoyant enough to drift with the current as it sinks," he explains. "You'll get bit more often if the bait approaches from the direction the fish expects food to come from, than if it plummets down from above."

By allowing the jig to drift naturally into openings in fallen trees, brush piles and other woody cover, you can tempt strikes from fish that would otherwise be impossible to reach. The technique requires a slow, precise presentation, so it may not be the best way to

---

Optimal Conditions in Tidal Rivers:

Season: post-spawn through mid-fall

Water Temperature: pattern holds until water drops below 60°F in fall

Weather: offshore wind

Water Stage: last 2 hours of out-going tide

Water Depth: 1 to 5 feet

Water Clarity: 2 feet or less

Time of Day: depends on tide

---

catch bass when they're active enough to chase lures passing outside the cover.

The locational patterns discussed here apply to the tidal rivers where Zaleski commonly fishes, but jig-drifting works in any good-sized river, assuming bass are relating to woody cover. The main difference in fishing tidal rivers is the constantly changing water level. It keeps bass on the move, and causes them to turn on and off more quickly and more often than bass in other waters.

Rich Zaleski

Hometown: Stevenson, Connecticut

Favorite Waters for Technique: Connecticut and Hudson rivers

Career Highlights: Winner: 1978 Northern Bass Anglers' Association Tournament of Champions; 1984 North American Bass Association Tournament of Champions and Angler of the Year

FLUCTUATING TIDES have a dramatic effect on bass location in tidal rivers. At high tide, look for bass (blue) scattered throughout marshes connected to the main river.

As low tide approaches, you'll find the fish (red) positioned along current breaks, where they can pick off food carried by water draining out of the marshes.

Understanding Tides

Tidal fluctuations result mainly from the moon's gravitational pull on the earth's surface (opposite). This pull creates a bulge of water that stays under the moon as the earth revolves. Centrifugal forces create another bulge of about the same magnitude on the side of the earth opposite the moon. The earth makes one revolution relative to the moon about every 25 hours, and during this time, a given point on the earth experiences a high tide as it passes under the moon, a low tide as it turns away from the moon, another high tide as it passes under the bulge opposite the moon, and another low tide as it turns toward the moon again.

Atlantic and Pacific coastal waters experience this typical pattern of two highs and lows every 25 hours; a low tide occurs about 6¼ hours after a high. But the shape of the ocean's basin and other geophysical factors sometimes interfere with the typical pattern. Consequently, some regions, such as the Gulf coast, experience only one high and one low every 25 hours; the low comes about 12½ hours after the high.

Tides vary considerably in different locations. Some places on earth have tides of 30 feet or more; in others, the tide is only 1 foot. And the amount of tidal fluctuation changes throughout the month. The greatest fluctuation (spring tide) takes place during the full moon and new moon; the smallest (neap tide), during the first- and last-quarter moon.

Weather conditions along the coast also affect water levels in the river. The levels are higher than normal with onshore winds; lower with offshore winds. Water levels are higher than normal with a low barometer; lower with a high barometer.

As the tide rises in coastal areas, salt water flows up coastal rivers. The higher the tide, the farther its effects extend upstream. Tidal peaks occur at different times at different points on the river. How fast the tide moves upstream depends on the configuration of the channel; the straighter and deeper it is, the faster the tide progresses.

The downstream reaches of tidal rivers are nearly as salty as seawater, the middle reaches are brackish and the upper reaches are fresh. The extent of tidal influence varies in different rivers, depending on the amount of stream flow, gradient of the river channel, and location of dams or waterfalls.

When and Where to Drift Jigs

The normal annual pattern for most river-dwelling bass is to spawn in still backwaters, then after spawning, move to a spot where current washes food to them. When the water temperature drops below 60°F in fall, they retreat to deep, slack-water holes where they spend the winter. The jig-drifting technique is effective only when bass are relating to current.

Most bass rivers are low in clarity, so the fish hold in shallow water, often less than 5 feet. If the clarity exceeds two feet, the fish tend to be warier, and more of them hold in deeper water.

In tidal rivers, you must pay close attention to the daily tide cycle. As a rule, bass are easiest to catch during the last two hours of the outgoing tide. The falling water forces them to abandon flooded marshes and creeks, and they move into deeper channels connecting to the main river or into the main river itself.

Bass forced out of a marsh or creek by falling water normally don't go far from the mouth. Look for them in small eddies that form behind a current break, such as a fallen tree, dock piling, weed bed or any projection or pocket along the shoreline that creates an eddy.

Fishing is usually slow at dead-low tide, when there is practically no current, but picks up again during the first hour or so of the incoming tide. The fish are still relating to the same current breaks, but facing the opposite direction. As the water continues to rise, however, baitfish move back into flooded creeks and marshes to get out of the current, and the bass follow. They're much more difficult to find when they're scattered in these large backwaters.

Any conditions that cause lower tides tend to improve fishing by further concentrating the bass around current breaks. Tides are lower during the full moon and new moon, for instance, than at other times of the month. You can identify prime low tides by referring to a weekly tide table.

Higher-than-normal tides, such as those caused by onshore winds, make fishing tough. High, muddy water caused by torrential rains also kills fishing.

One way anglers can improve their success is by moving upriver or downriver to avoid unfavorable tides or take advantage of favorable ones.

Before fishing a tidal river, check with local sources to learn what reach holds the most bass. As a rule, you won't find many bass downstream of the point where barnacles begin to appear, because the water is too salty. The lower part of the productive reach, however, usually produces the biggest bass.

In a high-gradient river, only the lower reaches are affected by tides. In a low-gradient river, however, the tidal influence may extend more than 100 miles upstream.

A dam or waterfall would prevent any tidal influence above that point, assuming the dam is higher than the tidal rise.

How the Moon Affects Tides

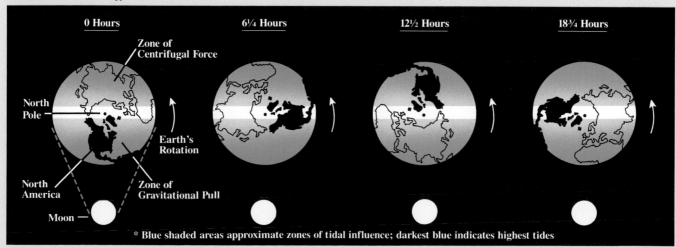

* Blue shaded areas approximate zones of tidal influence; darkest blue indicates highest tides

Exerpted (with modifications) from: Sternberg, D. 1990. Fishing Rivers & Streams. The Hunting & Fishing Library.

The Jig-Drifting Technique

The ideal way to drift a jig into a likely bass hangout is to position your boat in the current with the bow pointing upstream, while holding even with and just outside the cover. Then flip your jig far enough upstream of the cover so it reaches bottom just as it drifts into the fish's lie. Let the jig drift into the cover, then yo-yo it against the current by repeatedly pulling it back upstream and allowing it to drift into different pockets in the cover.

To achieve the proper drift, the weight of the jig and bulk of the trailer must be matched to the speed of the current (below). In very slow current, a jig that is too heavy won't drift at all. Fast current will blow away a jig that is too light, and it won't bounce along the bottom. Use a brushguard jig in a stand-up, rather than cone style, because it will hook more fish. Zaleski prefers dark colors, usually blacks, browns, blues, or combinations of them.

A long rod helps control the drift and reduce the amount of line needed to reach the cover. You'll normally use no more than 12 feet of line, measuring from the rod tip. The more line in the water, the more the current drag, and the less natural the presentation. Thin-diameter line also reduces current drag.

When you feel a strike, set the hook immediately and try to pull the fish upstream, away from the cover. Your drag should be tight so you can keep enough tension on the fish to prevent it from swimming back into the brushy tangle.

If you suspect the cover is holding bass, but they're not interested in your jig, try "finessing" them with a smaller lure and lighter line. Zaleski recommends a 4-inch lizard rigged Texas-style on an offset jig hook (below). You could also use a 4-inch worm, but a lizard is bulkier and the legs give it extra lift, so it will drift better. Using a 6½-foot, medium-power, fast-action spinning rod and 6- to 10-pound mono, drift the lure into the brush just as you would a heavier jig.

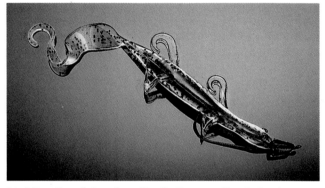

Mud Dog lizard rigged on Charlie Brewer offset jig hook

But this lighter jig may not be heavy enough to horse fish out of the cover. If the bass strikes outside the cover, set the hook right away and try to keep it from swimming back in. But if it strikes when the lure has drifted well into the cover, exert gentle pressure and try to lead the fish out *before* setting the hook.

"The reason jig drifting is so deadly is that you're taking advantage of the current rather than fighting it," Zaleski explains. "How else could you extract a stubborn bass from a current-swept brush pile?"

SELECT jigs based on current speed. In fast current, use a 7/16-ounce jig with a sparse skirt and a size 11 pork frog trailer (left). In slow current, try a 3/16-ounce jig with a bulkier skirt and a size 1 trailer (right).

How to Drift a Jig into Dense Cover

POSITION your boat even with or just upstream of the cover you want to fish. This way, you can easily drift a jig into the cover and pull fish out.

DRIFT the jig beneath the cover, then twitch it while feeding line. Each twitch allows current to wash the jig a little farther into the tangle.

SET the hook at an upstream angle and lead the fish upstream. If you attempt to pull the fish cross-current, it will probably foul in the cover.

Jig-drifting Tips

INCREASE flippin' distance by pulling out line between the first and second guides, rather than the first guide and the reel. This adds 2 to 3 feet to your flip.

LOOK for bass around old, algae-covered pilings, which attract aquatic insects and baitfish. New, pressure-treated pilings leach arsenic, which prevents algal growth.

SECURE a pork trailer, so it can't slide up the shank and foul the hook, by first threading on a grub body. A grub also adds bulk so the bait drifts better.

ADD a rattle to your jig when fishing in murky water. Slide a piece of shrink tubing over the hook shank, slip in a rattle and heat the tubing with a match.

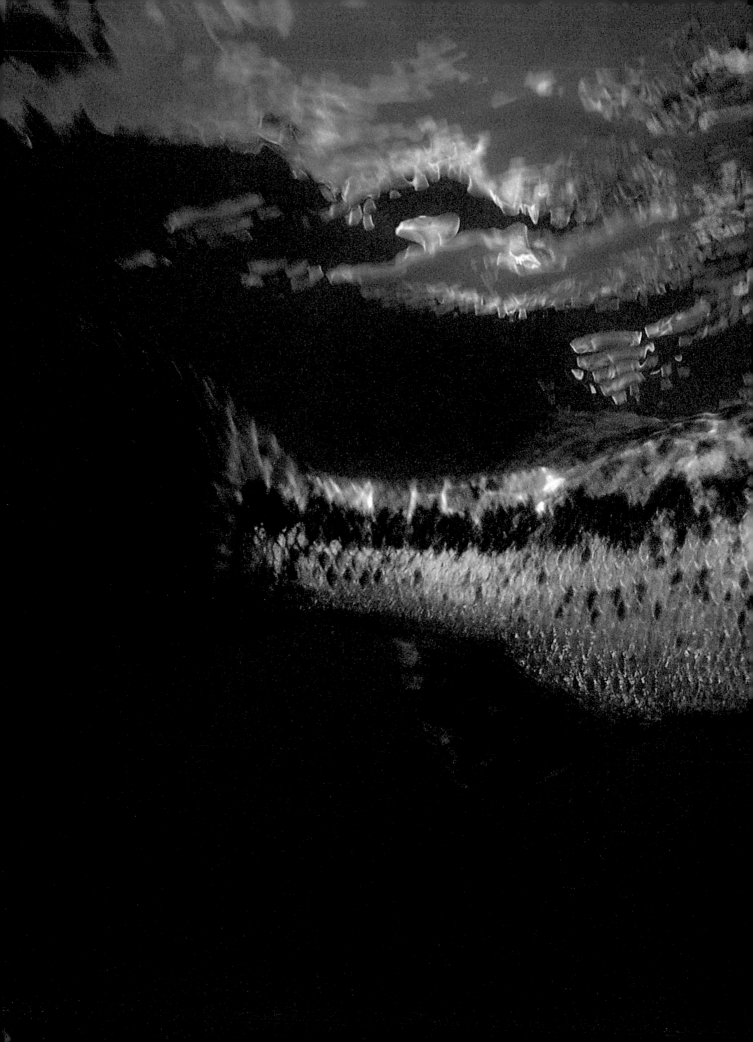

Advanced Plug Techniques

Zell's Topwater Tricks

Optimal Conditions:

Type of Water: any body of water with ample shallow-water bass habitat
Season: spring through fall
Water Temperature: above 55°F
Weather: cloudy and calm
Water Stage: stable or rising slowly
Water Depth: usually less than 5 feet, but sometimes deeper in clear lakes
Water Clarity: at least 1 foot
Time of Day: all day in cloudy weather; early and late in sunny weather

Ask an old-timer to recount his early bass-fishing memories, and he'll more than likely talk about lunkers slurping Hula Poppers or Jitterbugs off the surface around dawn or dusk. But you don't hear much topwater conversation among the modern generation of bass pros unless, of course, you're speaking with Zell Rowland – "Mr. Topwater."

Considered the best all-around topwater man in professional bass-fishing circles, Rowland to date has won nearly one million dollars using surface baits, far more than any other bass pro. "Lucky for me, most fishermen still think of topwaters strictly as morning and evening baits. I catch fish on 'em all day, sun or no sun. There's just something about a bait floundering on the surface that really turns the bass on."

When asked why more pros don't use topwaters, Rowland replied, "It takes a long time to learn to fish 'em, and each type of topwater has to be worked a little differently. Over the years, I've spent thousands of hours learning tricks that help me put fish in the boat.

"Course, topwaters aren't always the answer. You need lots of good shallow water cover and water tem-peratures above 55°F. If the water is too cold, too rough or too muddy, I usually go to other types of baits."

On the pages that follow, we'll show you Rowland's presentation strategies for each of his favorite types of topwaters. He rarely fishes a bait without somehow modifying it, so we've also included a complete collection of his personal bait-doctoring tips.

Zell Rowland

Hometown:
Montgomery, Texas
Favorite Waters for Technique:
Sam Rayburn Lake, Texas; Buggs Island Lake, Virginia/N. Carolina; Santee-Cooper Lake, S. Carolina
Career Highlights:
Winner: 1986 BASSMASTER Super-Invitational; 1991 Alabama BASSMASTER Invitational; 1992 Golden Blend Diamond Invitational World Bass Fishing Championship (all-time record prize of $150,000)

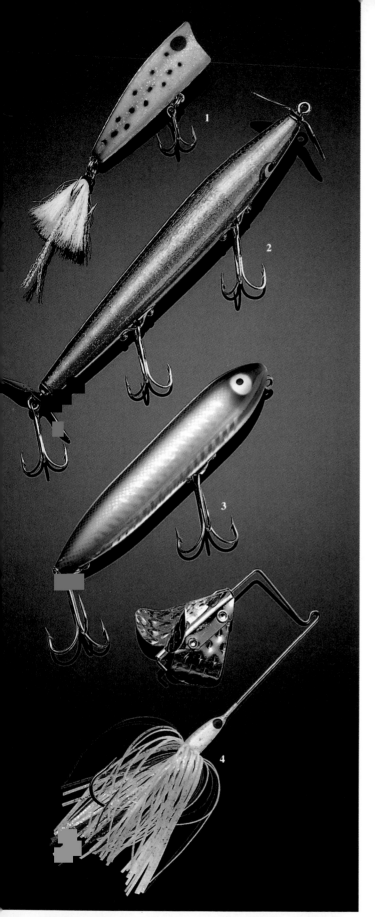

How to Fish Topwaters

Equipment:

Rod:

 for chuggers, propbaits and stickbaits: 6½-foot, medium-power, medium-action graphite baitcaster

 for buzzbaits: 7½-foot, medium-heavy-power, fast-action flippin' stick

Reel:

 for slow retrieves with chuggers: narrow-spool baitcaster with gear ratio of 4:1 or less

 for all other topwater retrieves: narrow-spool baitcaster with gear ratio of 5:1 to 6:1

Line: see individual lure sections

"You've got to let the fish tell you what they want on a given day," says Rowland. "Do they want a bait that makes more noise, or one that has a quieter, more subtle action? You have to have all the different topwaters and go through an elimination process.

"And there is no right or wrong way to fish a topwater. You have to vary your retrieve until the fish let you know the right combination of speed, intensity of twitches and time between them.

"The beauty of surface fishing is that you can see how the bait is working and how the fish are reacting. I start with a fast retrieve to cover some water, but if that's not working, I'll slow down. And if they don't like sharp twitches, I'll try gentle ones."

One of the most common mistakes in topwater fishing is setting the hook too soon and missing the fish (opposite). Rowland prefers a fairly soft rod that doesn't offer much resistance when a fish bites; this way, it will take the bait deeper.

A softer rod also helps in casting lightweight topwaters. It's important to make long casts, because bass in shallow water are easily spooked by angler movement and boat noise.

Another frequent mistake is attaching a topwater with a heavy snap-swivel, so the nose rides too low (opposite) and ruins the action. Line that is too light may also dampen a topwater's action, because it sinks faster than heavier line and causes you to pull the bait under when you twitch the rod.

Some of the baits Rowland uses require major modifications; others, only minor tinkering. He pays extremely close attention to little things when preparing his baits. For instance, he always replaces chrome hooks with high-quality bronze hooks (opposite), not only to improve his hooking percentage, but to ensure that the chrome doesn't spook fish on a sunny day.

ROWLAND'S FAVORITE TOPWATERS include chuggers, such as (1) Rebel Pop-R; propbaits, such as (2) Smithwick Devil's Horse; stickbaits, such as (3) Heddon Zara Spook; buzzbaits, such as (4) Strike King Buzz King.

Tips for Fishing Topwaters

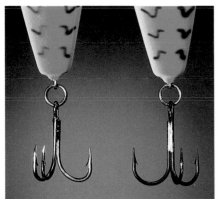

REPLACE thick-wire, chrome-plated, curved-point hooks (left) with extra-sharp, thin-wire, round-bend bronze hooks with straight points (right).

WAIT for the fish to pull the bait down before setting the hook (left). This increases your hooking percentage, because you're pulling the bait back into the fish. If you set too soon (right), you'll probably pull the bait away from the fish.

WATCH the bait very closely for any indication of a strike. Often, you won't see an obvious splash or swirl, just a slight ripple as the fish sucks the bait beneath the surface.

AVOID attaching the bait with a heavy clip or snap-swivel. The nose will sink (left) and the bait won't chug, walk or skitter as it should. Always tie directly to the attachment eye (right) so the nose is above water.

How to Reduce Backlashing

Everyone who uses baitcasting gear gets backlashes, or "professional overruns" as the pros jokingly call them. The problem is most serious with light baits, such as topwaters and unweighted soft plastics.

Many fishermen shy away from baitcasting gear to avoid the headache of untangling backlashes. Although there's no way to eliminate the problem, you can minimize it with the following steps:

•Try not to cast into the wind when using a light bait. The wind slows the flight of the bait, but the spool keeps spinning, producing a backlash.

•Select a narrow-spool reel. Because a narrow spool is lighter, it has much less momentum than a wide one, so it is less likely to backlash. And you'll find it easier to cast light baits with a narrow-spool reel.

•Adjust your spool tension properly. Here's a good rule: set the tension so the weight of the bait can barely turn the spool with the rod held horizontally.

•Learn to thumb the spool; even the best baitcasting reel will overrun once in a while if you don't. Depending on the reel you're using, you may have to feather the spool in mid-cast, and you must stop the spool with your thumb just before the bait hits the water.

•Don't throw the bait too hard. Cast with a smooth motion, letting the rod do the work. An intense arm motion gets the spool spinning too fast, so it's more likely to overrun.

•Make a long cast, then lay a strip of electrical tape over the spool. This eliminates severe backlashes, because the spool can overrun no deeper than the tape.

Tape spool to stop backlashes

•Don't overfill the spool with line; the line level should be no less than 1/8 inch from the top of the spool. The more line that comes off with each turn of the spool, the greater the chances for a backlash.

Chuggers

"I've thrown the Pop-R more than any other human being alive," Rowland contends. "If you use an ordinary Pop-R right out of the box, it makes a low-pitched chugging or burping noise, which isn't bad. But you'll catch a lot more fish if you sand it down."

Sanding (opposite) makes the bait float higher and at a different angle, about 45 degrees. So it's easier to skitter, has more lateral action and sounds like a shad flicking on the surface.

How to Fish a Pop-R

"It takes me almost two hours to sand one," Rowland says. "But they work so well, I've actually had guys steal them off my rods at weigh-ins." If you don't care to sand a Pop-R, select a "Pro" model. It has thinner walls, and an action more like a sanded one. But Rowland far prefers the action of his own sanded baits.

Start with a fast retrieve to mimic a skipping shad, but if that doesn't work, slow down. Make the head swish from side to side by throwing slack into the line between twitches. But don't expect as much lateral motion as you get with a stickbait.

Use 17- to 20-pound mono. Lighter line tends to sink, pulling the head down and resulting in a burping, rather than skipping, sound. But 12- to 14-pound line may be needed in clear water or when using a slower retrieve, because the fish may be line-shy.

CAST toward likely cover, then begin your retrieve with the rod at an angle of about 45 degrees. This will keep your line up so it can't sink.

SET THE HOOK with a firm sweep. With the small hooks, you don't want to jerk too hard. Set at whatever position the rod is in when the fish strikes.

LOWER the rod as the bait nears the boat. You'll get more splash (inset) with the rod tip low, and you won't pull the nose of the bait out of the water.

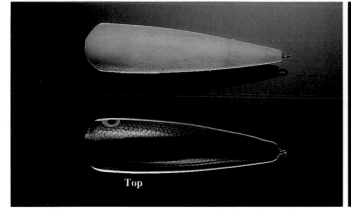

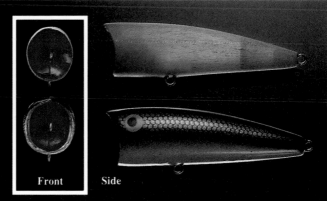

REMOVE the hooks. Using 60-grit sandpaper, sand the bait evenly until it tapers smoothly from front to back. Sand the belly only enough to remove the paint; do not sand the cupped face. Use emery cloth to smooth the surface. The sanded bait should have a smaller bulge in the middle than an unsanded one (top view) and a smaller hump on the back (side view). The edge of the cupped face should be much sharper (front view). The bait should be so thin you can feel it give when you squeeze it and you can see light through it.

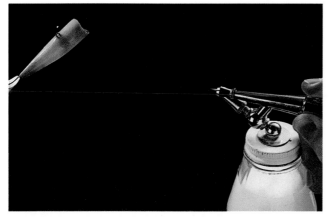

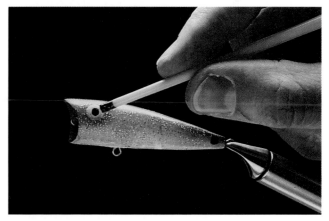

PAINT the sanded bait to match the predominant baitfish. An olive-green back and pearl belly, for instance, is a good match for shad. Sprinkle glitter onto the wet paint, if desired.

DAB on eyes and body spots using tapered handles of small paintbrushes. Cut off one handle at a wide spot for dabbing on eyes; another, near the tip, for the pupils. For round spots, the ends must be perfectly flat.

SPRAY the painted bait with clear lacquer to protect the finish and strengthen the thin walls.

REPLACE the rear hook, which is dressed with bucktail, with a better-quality bronze hook (p. 59) dressed with feathers similar in color to the forage. Tie six 1- to 1½-inch feathers to the hook, two per gap, so they curve outward. The feathers give you a more enticing action.

Propbaits

When bass are holding tight to cover, especially in murky water, Rowland relies heavily on a propbait. His favorite is the Smithwick Devil's Horse, which has propellers at opposite ends to create a lot of commotion. It may take the noise of a propbait to draw the fish out.

Propbaits are normally fished with a twitch-and-pause retrieve, varying speed and length of twitches, and the duration between them. To get the most from a propbait, you should modify the blades for different types of retrieves (below).

Use 17- to 20- pound mono with twin-bladed propbaits. Lighter line is limper and tends to curl around the front propeller. For smaller propbaits with a single rear propeller, use 12- to 14-pound mono.

Some propbaits have the old-style hook hangers that restrict hook movement. Remove them and substitute screw eyes and split rings, as you would with a stickbait (opposite).

How to Modify a Propbait for the Conditions

*STANDARD PROPBAIT.
Best for normal fishing
conditions*

*PROP BLADES BENT
FORWARD. Best for finicky
bass, because the bait does
not move forward as much
when you twitch it*

*REVERSED END FOR END.
Helps casting accuracy and
distance in windy weather,
because the bait has a more
aerodynamic shape*

*FRONT PROP REMOVED.
Gives the bait more of a side-
to-side "walking" action, for
extra attraction under tough
conditions*

Stickbaits

In extremely clear water, Rowland often uses a stickbait, his favorites being the Heddon Zara Spook, and its smaller cousin, the Zara Puppy.

"A Zara Spook is one of the world's best big fish baits," he contends. It's balanced and tapered exactly right for the enticing "walk-the-dog" retrieve, riding with the nose slightly out of the water for maximum lateral action.

The secret to getting good side-to-side action from a Zara, or any other stickbait, is to throw slack into the line after each twitch (below), so there is no resistance to lateral motion.

To get maximum action out of a Zara, however, you'll have to make some modifications, like repositioning the attachment eye (below). Use 17- to 20-pound mono with a Zara Spook; 12- to 14- with a Puppy. Line that's too heavy restricts the action.

"Zaras are one of the worst baits for holding fish," Rowland says. "The old-style hook hangers work like a crowbar in a door, so a fish can get the leverage it needs to throw the hook. Be sure to replace these hook hangers with split rings and screw eyes (below). Then, if they touch it, they're hung."

How to Doctor and Work a Stickbait

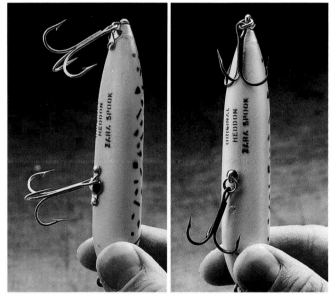

REPLACE old-style hook hangers (left) that restrict movement of the hooks, making it easy for bass to throw the bait. Substitute screw eyes and split rings (right), which will not allow the hooks to bind.

WALK THE DOG in a wide "Z" pattern by throwing slack into the line after each twitch. This way, the bait can glide freely to the side after the twitch, and you'll get a sharper jerk on the next twitch.

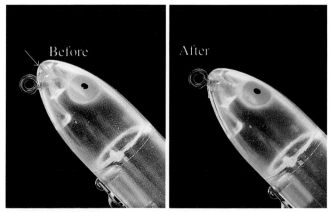

REPOSITION the front screw eye to make walking the dog easier. Drill a small hole halfway between the hole at the tip of the nose (arrow) and the old screw eye, and switch the eye to the new hole.

VEER your bait toward cover by alternating soft and hard twitches. It will glide farther one way than the other, so you can lead it in the desired direction. To help the bait veer to one side, bend the front screw eye the opposite way (inset).

BUZZBAIT STYLES. Safety-pin buzzers (left) have an L-shaped arm extending above the body to support the blade; in-line buzzers (right) have the blade on the main shaft. The in-line style rides higher in the water, so it's a better choice for fishing over matted weeds. But you can modify a safety-pin bait so the blade clacks on the main shaft (opposite), making it noisier, and because it rides lower in the water, it tends to hook fish better.

Buzzbaits

Buzzbaits are a good choice for locating fish, because you can cast them farther and retrieve them faster than most other topwaters. They work well around dense cover because of the single, upturned hook. They come in two basic styles: safety-pin and in-line (above).

"I like a ¼- or ½-ounce buzzbait," Rowland says. "Don't pay much attention to blade style – any blade is fine, just so it makes a lot of racket." To make the bait louder, he files grooves in the rivet or adds a "clacker" (opposite). He prefers old baits to new ones, because the blade tends to squeak more as it becomes worn.

Rowland usually adds a single-hook trailer to his buzzbait, because he feels his hooking percentage is too low with only the main hook. In dense weeds, the trailer is turned up so it won't foul as easily. In light cover, it's turned down to improve hooking odds and increase the chances of hooking the fish in the lower jaw, so they're less inclined to jump and throw the hook. Removing the skirt (opposite) also improves your hooking percentage, especially when the fish are fussy, because they tend to strike farther forward on the bait.

Start fishing a buzzbait at medium to fast speed. Using a fast-action flippin' stick (p. 58) and 20-pound mono, make a long cast and begin reeling immediately, with your rod top held high. The long rod improves casting distance, makes it easier to steer the bait around cover, and helps keep the head of the bait riding high when you start the retrieve. Gradually lower the rod tip as the bait nears the boat; otherwise, you'll pull the head too far out of the water, and the blade won't spin properly. You may get more strikes if you shake the bait periodically during the retrieve.

If the fish aren't responding to a rapid retrieve, try slowing down. To get the blades to turn at this slow speed, cup them a little more (opposite). Sometimes, bass will only hit a bait when it stops. A buzzbait is not a good choice when the fish are in this kind of mood, because it sinks when you stop reeling.

When a fish grabs the bait, hesitate until you feel resistance before setting the hook, just as you would with other topwaters. Because of the heavier hook on a buzzbait, however, you'll have to pop the rod a little harder to sink the barb.

Rowland's topwater prowess is a direct result of his dedication to topwater fishing and his attention to detail. "I'm constantly taking baits apart and putting them back together to see what makes them work," he explained. "And I'm always trying new ways of doctoring baits and new retrieves. Most guys aren't willing to spend the time. They take a bait out of the box, make ten casts and put it away. Whether it's a Pop-R or any other topwater, you've got to completely understand the bait if you want to catch fish consistently."

How to Modify a Buzzbait

REMOVE the rivet (arrow) holding on the buzzblade, then file grooves in it as shown in the inset, and reassemble. The blade spinning against the grooved rivet makes a lot of commotion. For even more noise, replace the standard aluminum rivet with a steel rivet that has been grooved. Another way to add noise: bend the shaft so the edge of the blade just ticks it.

ADD a "clacker" by removing the buzzblade and sliding some beads, a clevis and a Colorado blade onto the vertical arm. Replace the buzzblade; when it turns, it will clack against the Colorado blade.

ADJUST the amount of blade cupping to accommodate different retrieve speeds. The slower the retrieve, the more the blade must be cupped to keep it spinning.

DRILL holes in a buzzblade as shown; the holes leave a bubble trail in the water, which helps draw bass. Also, a bait with drilled blades does not veer to the side as much as a standard model.

 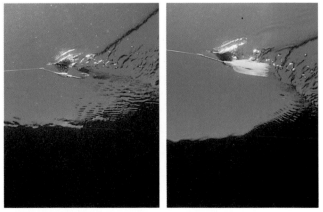

SELECT a buzzbait with a flat head (left) when you want to retrieve more slowly. The flattened shape planes the bait upward much more than a standard head (right).

REMOVE the skirt from your buzzbait (left) when you're getting too many short strikes. With the skirt in place (right), the bait's center of attention is farther to the rear, so a fish is more likely to strike behind the hook.

Crankin' the Weeds for Largemouth

Optimal Conditions:

Type of Water: weedy natural lakes

Season: post-spawn through fall

Water Temperature: effective until water temperature drops below 45°F in fall

Cover Type: edges of dense submerged weedbeds

Weather: warm, overcast, moderate wind

Water Stage: normal

Water Depth: 20 feet or less

Water Clarity: at least 3 feet

Time of Day: anytime there is a moderate wind

If you've ever tried fishing a crankbait in a weedy lake, chances are you didn't do it for long – unless picking weeds off hooks is your idea of a good time.

When faced with dense weeds, most bass fishermen select other lures, such as spinnerbaits or weedless jigs. But Tom Fudally doesn't see the weeds as a problem. "I love to throw cranks in these lakes. Don't know of any method that will put a limit into the boat faster.

"A crankbait covers more water in less time than any other type of lure, and it will often draw 'reaction' strikes from neutral bass. Sometimes a crankbait will activate what I call the 'Judas bass,' because it divulges the location of a whole school. And when one fish strikes, it often activates the rest of them."

When you cover this much water, you not only find the active fish, you find the right vegetation and bottom type. If you suspect fish are in the area but they're not biting, you can work them with a slower, more thorough bait, such as a weedless jig or Texas-rigged worm.

Another advantage to crankbaits: they're a good choice in windy weather, when it's hard to fish jigs, worms or other baits that require a deft touch to achieve the right action and detect strikes.

Fudally, who used crankbaits to win the prestigious Don Shelby U.S. Invitational on Minnesota's Lake Minnetonka in 1989, likes to use crankbaits whenever bass are holding along or just outside the weedline or over the weedtops. They're not a good choice when the fish are tucked into deep weeds.

On the pages that follow, we'll show you when and where to use crankbaits in weed-infested lakes, the equipment you need and the most productive techniques.

Tom Fudally

Hometown:
Maple Grove, Minnesota
Favorite Waters for Technique:
Lake Minnetonka, Gull Lake, Lake Miltona, Lake Waconia and Le Homme Dieu chain, all in Minnesota
Career Highlights:
Winner, 1989 Don Shelby U.S. Invitational; Muskie lure designer and former owner of Fudally Tackle Company; Muskies, Inc., Hall of Famer

When and Where to Use Crankbaits in Weedy Lakes

Conditions that cause bass to become active – warm weather, overcast skies, and wind – are ideal for crankbait fishing any time of year. When the skies are clear and the water calm, you'll do best around dawn and dusk. Crankin' is least effective under cold-front conditions, because bass tuck deep into the weeds and won't move as far to take a bait.

As a rule, crankin' works best at water temperatures of 55°F or higher, but it will catch bass at temperatures as low as 45°. Where you find bass in weedy lakes and how you fish them varies, however, depending mainly on the height of the weeds (below).

SHORT WEEDS. Many weeds, such as coontail, form a blanket on the bottom from a few inches to a few feet thick. The weedtops are exposed only near shore. The most active bass cruise near the weedtops or along the weedline; inactive bass bury themselves deep in the weeds.

TALL WEEDS. Weeds such as cabbage grow to the surface in water as much as 15 feet deep. Active bass patrol inside turns and points along the weedline, particularly points with a clean, hard-bottomed lip tapering into deep water. Inactive bass usually retreat several feet into the weeds.

Techniques for Crankin' the Weeds

Equipment:
Rod: 6½- to 7-foot, medium-action, medium-power baitcaster, either graphite or fiberglass
Reel: low-gear-ratio (less than 4.5:1) baitcaster with longer-than-normal reel handle for extra cranking power
Line: 10-pound-test mono for smaller lures; 12-pound for larger ones
Lures: medium- to deep-running crankbaits

"There's a lot more to crankin' than tossing out a bait and reeling it in," Fudally says. "Pay attention to your boat position and retrieve on every cast. If you allow your mind to drift, you'll catch more weeds than bass."

Crankbait selection is also critical. Not only must you choose a lure that runs at precisely the correct depth, its color and action must suit the water clarity and the mood of the bass. There is no sure way to predict which lure will work best, but the following guidelines will help.

The design of the lip (opposite) affects running depth, as does line diameter. A deep-running crankbait will lose about a foot of depth for every .001-inch increase in line diameter. Shallower-running lures will lose proportionately less. And with thicker line, it takes longer for the lure to reach its maximum running depth.

The best colors vary from one body of water to another, but bright or fluorescent colors generally work best in dirty water; dull or natural ones in clear water. Most anglers believe a wide wobble is best in warm water, but the reverse is actually true. A lure with a wide wobble or lots of "roll" (opposite) is most effective in cold water, because it still has adequate action at a slow retrieve speed. A lure with a tighter wiggle and less roll works better in warm water, because it's easier to retrieve faster.

Detecting strikes is seldom a problem when fishing crankbaits, but it can be in weedy lakes. Sometimes bass merely grab the lure and hold on, giving you the impression you've hooked a weed. To be safe, set the hook when you feel anything out of the ordinary. The fine-wire trebles penetrate easily, so you don't need a powerful hook set. Crank-set the hook by reeling faster while making a smooth sweep with your rod.

A bass can throw a crankbait more easily than a single-hook lure, like a jig or spinnerbait. But you can minimize the chances of losing the fish by playing it properly. After setting the hook, pull horizontally to get the fish away from the weeds. If you hold the rod high and pull vertically, you'll bring the fish to the surface where it can easily throw the lure. If you see the line start to move up rapidly, plunge your rod into the water while keeping pressure on the fish. This reduces the chances it will jump, and the angle of pull keeps the hooks buried. A word of caution: don't set your drag too tight or attempt to horse a crankbait-hooked bass. The trebles tear out easily, especially when a fish makes a last-minute run.

Don't try to lip-land a bass with a crankbait in its mouth. Instead, keep the line taut, put your hand under its belly and quickly lift it into the boat.

Land crankbait-hooked bass like this

To successfully fish crankbaits in weedy lakes, tailor your strategy to the weed-growth pattern as shown on the following page.

Principles of Crankbait Design

Typical lip angle on (a) deep-, (b) medium- and (c) shallow-running crankbaits

With thousands of crankbait models on the market, it helps to be able to look at one and have a pretty good idea of how it will perform. Below are the major considerations:

LIP. The length, width and angle of the lip determine a bait's running depth. The longer and wider the lip, and the straighter it extends off the nose, the deeper the lure will track.

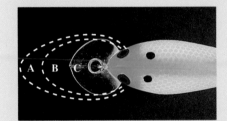

Typical lip size on (a) deep-, (b) medium- and (c) shallow-running crankbaits

The lip also affects side-to-side action. The wider the lip, the more wobble; the more angle, the more roll.

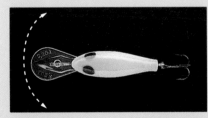

Wobble is movement sideways to the lengthwise axis

Roll is pivoting movement around the lengthwise axis

A crankbait with a large, straight lip is the best choice in snaggy cover. The lip runs interference for the hooks, and the straight angle causes the lure to run nose-down, so the hooks aren't as likely to bump the cover.

A bait's action depends on the position of the line-attachment eye on the lip, as well. The closer to the nose, the more the bait tends to roll.

WEIGHTING. Most crankbaits have little or no added weight, so they float at rest. But some have lead inserts, so they sink or are neutrally buoyant. Sinking baits can be counted down to any depth. Neutrally buoyant ones can be retrieved very slowly, without floating up, so they're a good choice when fish are sluggish.

BODY MATERIAL. The type of body material affects a crankbait's action and flotation. Common materials include:

•Plastic. Most crankbaits are made of hard or foamed plastic. Hard-plastic models, the most common type, are much more durable. The hard, hollow shell makes them best suited for rattles. Foamed-plastic models are lighter and more "responsive." Assuming a foamed-plastic bait is identical in shape and weighted the same as a hard-plastic, it would ride higher in the water, have livelier action, respond better to a twitching-style retrieve and be easier to fish above weedtops or float off of snags.

•Wood. Balsa and cedar are the most common types of wood used for crankbaits. Balsa is the lightest and most responsive, but cedar is much more durable. Wooden crankbaits are usually more costly than plastic ones.

SHAPE. The body shape of a crankbait also affects its action. Thin-bodied models generally have a tight, rapid wiggle; fat-bodied types, a wider, slower wobble. Deep-diving models usually have a fat body; a thin one does not run as true and is more difficult to keep in tune.

Techniques for Short Weeds

Select a crankbait that tracks at about the same depth as the weedtops. Experiment with different casting angles, lures, retrieve speeds and rod positions (opposite) until you find the combination that keeps the lure barely tickling the weedtops.

If the weeds taper gradually, for instance, position your boat in deep water, cast perpendicular to the break so the lure lands in shallower water, and retrieve so it follows the weedtops. But if the weeds slope sharply into deep water, cast parallel to the break; this way, your lure will have more time to dive to the level of the fish.

Cast at a right angle to the break in gradually sloping weeds

For each crankbait, there is an optimum speed at which it tracks deepest. Faster or slower, and the lure will run shallower. If possible, keep your retrieve on the slow side in early and late season, when the water temperature is cool.

During each retrieve, carefully note when you start to feel weeds. When you feel the first tick, stop reeling, give the lure slack so it can float up a few inches, then reel again. This stop-and-go retrieve usually works better than a steady one, especially in early season.

Subsequent casts at slightly different angles will reveal relative water depth and weed height. If you start bumping weeds earlier in your retrieve, the water is shallower; if you feel them later, it's deeper.

Techniques for Tall Weeds

With the weeds growing to or just beneath the surface, it's nearly impossible to retrieve a crankbait over the weedtops without fouling. You must run the lure nearly parallel to the weedline and get it close to the bottom. The technique, which Fudally calls, "crankin' the wall," is best done by using deep- or super-deep-diving crankbaits.

Crankin' the wall

The key to catching bass along a wall of weeds is finding the perfect casting angle. Instead of holding your boat over deep water and casting toward the weeds, hold it right over the deep edge of the weeds, angle your cast slightly away from the weedline and retrieve so the bait just bumps the weed edge at its maximum running depth. This way, you'll catch bass holding at the base of the weedline or on the clean lip.

If you cast exactly parallel to the weedline, the lure will bump weeds too soon and probably foul. If you angle your cast too far out from the weedline, you won't bump weeds until too late in the retrieve.

Reel rapidly as soon as the lure hits the water; this way, it will get down in a hurry. Once you feel it tick the weeds, slow down. The lure will stay at the same depth, and the slower speed will usually draw more strikes. Under ideal feeding conditions, however, you may get more strikes with a faster retrieve.

The water resistance from a super-deep-diving crankbait can wear you out in a hurry. But a reel with a low gear ratio (less than 4.5:1) and a long handle minimizes the effort required, enabling you to fish for extended periods with little fatigue.

You can adjust your bait's running depth by changing the distance you hold your rod tip above the water. If you're having trouble getting the lure to run deep enough, push the rod tip into the water. This will give you as much as three feet more depth. If you still aren't bumping weeds, select a deeper-running lure or use thinner-diameter line.

"The best way to learn how to crank the weeds is to go out and try it," Fudally advises. "And don't give up because you're dragging in lots of weeds and few fish. Bass in these lakes seldom see crankbaits – once you learn how to use them, they can be your ace in the hole."

How to Work an Unfamiliar Weedy Point

PLACE markers around an unfamiliar point so you can easily crankbait the weed-line on either side. First, mark (A) the tip of the point, then (B and C) the edges. Once you become familiar with the point, the markers are no longer necessary.

Crankbait-fishing Tips

TIE your line to the split ring so neither the knot nor the attachment eye rests in the ring's gap (arrow), damaging the line or restricting the action.

KICK in a marker when you hook a bass. This way, you can keep fishing, you maintain your casting angle, and the wind won't blow you off the spot.

USE a net with plastic-coated mesh when crankbait fishing. The hooks won't penetrate the weave, and the stiff mesh won't ball up on the hook.

Weighted Stickbaits: Rx for Coldwater Bass

Stickbaits, jerkbaits, minnow plugs – it makes no difference what you call them – these lifelike minnow imitations have long been standard items in the tackle boxes of most freshwater anglers.

The first minnow plug was imported to the United States from Finland in 1959 by Ron Weber, now President of the Normark Corporation. "At first, I couldn't get the tackle industry to take the Rapala seriously," Weber recalled. "A store owner would pick one up and hand it right back. Too light to cast, he'd say. That was probably true with the heavy line they used back in those days. But as lighter tackle and lines became popular, the lures began to catch on. It soon became obvious they were terrific baits for practically any kind of gamefish."

A slow, steady retrieve gives the lure a unique wobble that closely mimics a swimming shiner. After these lures were introduced, bass fishermen quickly added a retrieve variation. They found that the plug's high buoyancy made it possible to use an erratic, twitch-and-pause surface retrieve that worked magic on shallow-water bass. When given a sharp twitch, the lure dives a few inches, then quickly pops back to the surface, where bass strike it at rest. This retrieve has now become a standard bass-fishing technique.

Innovative southern anglers added yet another effective twist. They discovered that the twitch-and-pause retrieve worked considerably better with the lure weighted to make it neutrally buoyant. This way, it would "hang" in the face of the fish, rather than immediately floating up – a major advantage in tempting uninterested bass to strike. The weighted stickbait technique is the focus of this article.

Optimal Conditions:

Type of Water: any reservoir with fairly clear water
Season: winter through pre-spawn
Water Temperature: 40 to 60°F
Weather: winter: sunny days; pre-spawn: cloudy, windy days
Water Stage: any stage
Water Depth: bass must be within 12 feet of the surface
Water Clarity: at least 2 feet
Time of Day: afternoon

Stacey King, a professional bass angler from Reeds Spring, Missouri, began using weighted stickbaits in nearby mountain lakes, such as Table Rock and Bull Shoals. Now he uses them regularly on the B.A.S.S. tour. "Found out about 'em years ago when some guys from Oklahoma and Arkansas came up here and started winning tournaments on Table Rock. They just drilled a hole in the bait and let it fill with water.

"It's definitely a big-bass technique. When the water's cold, a hawg bass just doesn't want to chase – you've got to put the bait right in its face. That's when a weighted stickbait really shines."

King, generally considered "the stickbait man" in pro bass circles, has perfected the weighting technique to get maximum performance from his lures. "The idea is to make it look like an injured baitfish," he says. "It's a visual deal – they see a quick flash, like a shad struggling to right itself, and they run up and hit it."

Stacey King

Hometown:
Reeds Spring, Missouri
Favorite Waters for Technique:
Table Rock and Bull Shoals lakes
Career Highlights:
Qualified for BASS Masters Classic 5 out of 6 years, from 1989 to 1994
Guided 25 years on Ozark Mountain lakes

When and Where to Use
Weighted Stickbaits

Weighted stickbaits are most effective at water temperatures from 40 to 60°F, particularly from late winter through the pre-spawn period. In winter, however, it takes sunny weather to activate the bass and draw them up into stickbait range, which generally means a depth of 12 feet or less. The fish don't move horizontally to reach shallow water, they simply rise vertically to feed on baitfish drawn to the sun-warmed surface layer.

Because the weighted stickbait technique relies on visual attraction, it's most productive in waters where visibility is at least 2 feet. King does most of his stickbait fishing in deep, clear reservoirs, but the technique can be used in any man-made or natural lake with adequate clarity.

The exact location of the bass depends on the type of water you're fishing. In Ozark Mountain lakes, for instance, most bass spend the winter relating to sharp-breaking structure along the main river channel or major creek channels. They move vertically along the steep breaks, rising to depths of 5 to 15 feet on warm days and dropping into 25 feet or more on cold days.

Structure with flooded timber is most likely to hold largemouth. The fish suspend high in the branches in warm, stable weather and use deep branches under cold-front conditions.

As the water starts to warm in spring, bass move up on the structure, feeding on shallow flats adjacent to the steep breaks where they spent the winter. Cold fronts may push them back to the steep breaks. As spring progresses, they begin working their way toward the small coves and shoreline pockets where they will spawn.

Cloudy, windy weather is better once the fish begin moving to the vicinity of their spawning areas. Choppy water makes them less wary, and they feed aggressively along windswept shorelines, where windblown plankton draws and collects baitfish.

The technique's effectiveness fades by the onset of spawning, which usually begins a few weeks earlier in the creek arms than in the main lake coves.

Weighted stickbaits work well not only for largemouth, but also for smallmouth and spotted bass. But the locational patterns vary somewhat for the three species. Largemouth can be found on suitable structure throughout the lake, even ranging into the back ends of small creek arms. But smallmouth inhabit only the main basin and large creek arms. Spots have intermediate locational tendencies.

Weighted stickbaits produce a mixed bag of largemouth (left), smallmouth (center) and spotted (right) bass

UNDERWATER EXTENSIONS. Gradually sloping points often have long underwater extensions or large flats projecting from their tips. The most productive extensions or flats have plenty of 5- to 20-foot-deep water.

PEA-GRAVEL POINTS. Pre-spawn bass seek out a pea-gravel bottom for spawning. They stage on gradual points with this type of bottom, then move into nearby shoreline pockets with the same type of bottom to spawn.

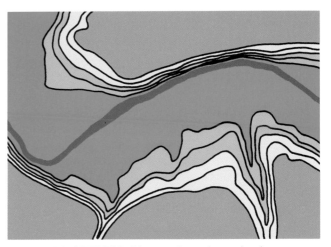

CHANNEL SWINGS. Places where the main-river or creek channel abut a steep shoreline concentrate bass in winter. The fish prefer staying close to the break when making their vertical movements.

CHUNK-ROCK POINTS. Points with plenty of large, broken rocks usually indicate a sharp-sloping breakline. They attract bass, particularly largemouth and spots, during the winter months.

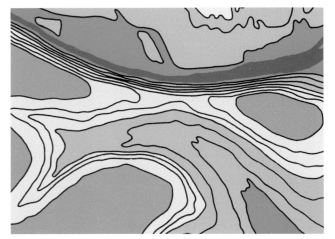

SADDLES. Underwater connections, or saddles, between structural elements, such as a point and island, draw all three bass species. The most productive saddles level off at 10 to 20 feet.

Techniques for Fishing Weighted Stickbaits

Equipment:

Rod:
 for open water: 6½-foot, medium- to medium-heavy-power, fast-action, long-handled baitcaster
 for woody cover: 5½-foot, pistol-grip baitcaster with same power and action
Reel: baitcaster with gear ratio no higher than 5:1
Line:
 for light cover: 8- to 10-pound, low-vis, abrasion-resistant mono
 for heavy cover: 12- to 17-pound, low-vis, abrasion-resistant mono

---

A glance at Stacey King's tackle box reveals a wide selection of weighted stickbaits, consisting of shallow (less than 5 feet), medium (4 to 8 feet) and deep (more than 8 feet) runners. But deep runners normally aren't needed in clear water, because a medium runner will pull the deep fish up.

"When I'm fishing over weedy or brushy cover, I use plugs that are just a little less than neutrally buoyant," King says. "This way, they rise slowly when you stop reeling, so they'll float away from the cover. But when cover is not a concern, I prefer a bait that suspends motionless. I may even use a sinking plug if I'm trying to reach deep water.

"Weighting is a painstaking process. I like to drill a hole, insert a lead tube and leave a little extra sticking out. Then I can keep filing it off until the weight is perfect." King weights most plugs in the belly, but some have internal wire connectors, so they must be weighted in the side or top.

"Most people don't realize that water temperature changes a plug's buoyancy. The colder the water, the more weight you need. If you're going to be fishing in cold water, test your bait in cold water."

Water temperature is also important in selecting plug size. As a rule, King prefers 5-inch baits in water of 50°F or less; 5½- to 7-inchers in water warmer than 50°.

Using a long-handled rod for extra casting distance and keeping the wind at your back, make a long cast and reel quickly to get the plug down to, or just above, the level of the fish. Then slow down and retrieve as shown below; a reel with a low gear ratio keeps you from reeling too fast. When you're fishing in standing timber, a shorter, pistol-grip rod is a better choice because you can cast more accurately.

You may have to experiment to find the presentation that best suits the mood of the fish. Try starting with a basic stop-and-go retrieve. With your rod tip low, twitch the bait sharply to make it dart and flash, then hesitate a few seconds. That's when most fish will strike. Vary the hesitation length; you may have to wait as long as 30 seconds between twitches, but sometimes a series of steady twitches works best. If sharp twitches aren't working, try 3- to 5-foot sweeps. Or, combine sweeps with twitches.

Bass may hit the lure hard, or you may just feel a subtle tick or a little extra weight. Crank-set the hook by making a firm, sideways sweep and reeling faster.

Weighted stickbaits are no longer the secret they once were, and as preweighted models become available from manufacturers, their popularity is likely to soar. Stacey King's advice: "If you like to catch big bass, this is a technique you need to perfect and add to your fishing arsenal."

How to Retrieve a Weighted Stickbait

TWITCH the lure one to three times, after reeling it to the desired depth. The more active the fish, the harder and faster the twitches should be.

PAUSE after twitching, letting the line go slack. If there is any tension on the line, the bait will continue to glide forward.

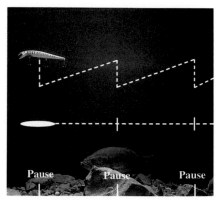

UNWEIGHTED baits (top) float up during pauses, away from sluggish fish. Weighted ones (bottom) track deeper and stay at the same depth.

How to Weight a Stickbait

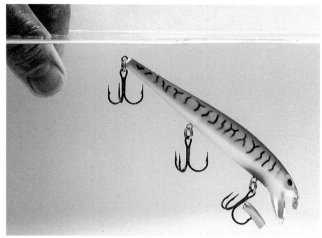

HANG a piece of lead tubing on the front hook, and trim the weight so the plug barely sinks.

SINK the plug with a weighted noose. Move the noose so the plug floats as shown; mark noose position on belly.

DRILL a hole at the mark on the plug's belly. Dab in epoxy glue. Implant lead so it protrudes slightly.

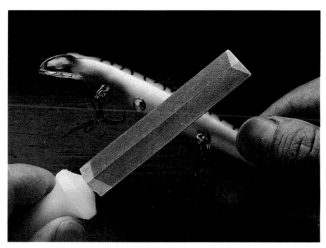

FILE off the lead until you achieve the desired buoyancy, then cover the lead with epoxy glue.

Other Weighting Methods

WRAP hooks with lead wire or solder to achieve the right buoyancy. Try to keep the wire from filling the hook gap, reducing the "bite."

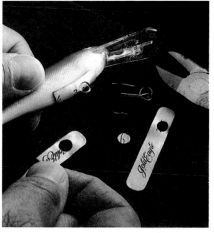

APPLY strips of golfer's tape to the bottom of the plug to achieve the desired buoyancy. Seal in the tape with epoxy glue.

REMOVE rubber inserts from Rubber-cor sinkers. Pinch one onto the front hook and a smaller one onto the middle. Trim lead for correct buoyancy.

Breaking the Live-Bait Habit for Trophy Largemouth

Optimal Conditions:

Type of Water: deep, clear California water-supply reservoirs
Season: late fall through early spring
Water Temperature: 47 to 60°F
Water Depth: 25 feet or less
Water Stage: normal, stable
Water Clarity: moderately clear
Weather: overcast
Time of Day: early morning, late afternoon

Much of what we read about trophy-bass fishing these days involves some kind of live bait. In Florida, for instance, anglers traditionally use foot-long golden shiners to pull the big females off their spawning beds. In Texas, trophy hunters catch the spawners on waterdogs. In California, now the nation's top giant-bass producer, trophy specialists have learned to entice finicky biters with live crayfish (p. 25).

Not only are some of these live-bait tactics controversial from a conservation standpoint, many bass anglers simply don't like fishing this way. While you could argue that nothing else catches trophy bass like live bait, California anglers are using some techniques that aren't far behind.

Troy Folkestad, a California guide and big-bass specialist, takes a good share of his trophies on a unique type of jointed minnow plug.

Called the A.C. Plug, the huge bait has the size, action and color of a stocked rainbow trout, a favorite of these giant bass. The halves of the plug clack together, producing much more noise than other lures.

Randy Best, a successful tournament pro who spends a good share of his time plying southern California lakes, prefers a football jig similar to, but lighter than, that used for jigging the steep bluff walls of canyon reservoirs (p. 46). The football-shaped head gives the lure a natural, crayfishlike action.

The advantage of the plug over the jig is that you can retrieve it much faster and work the spots more quickly. But if the bass aren't in a chasing mood, you can work the jig right in their face. Although these methods were developed on southern California lakes, they have good potential in most other trophy-bass waters.

Troy Folkestad

Hometown:
Mission Viejo, California
Favorite Waters for Technique:
Castaic and Casitas Lakes, California
Career Highlights:
Big bass specialist; 31 ten-pound-plus bass; one-day, five-fish catch weighing 47.6 pounds

Randy Best

Hometown:
Norco, California
Favorite Waters for Technique:
Lakes Mead and Havasu, on Colorado River; Lake Shasta, California
Career Highlights:
Winner: 1991 WON BASS California Delta Invitational; 1994 WON BASS Lake Mead Invitational

Where and When to Catch Trophy California Bass

California's biggest bass come from deep, clear lakes that have been stocked with Florida-strain largemouth. Of the state's fifty-plus Florida-bass lakes, the very best trophy producers (map below) are primarily in the southern one-third of the state, where the growing season is considerably longer than in northern California. Another requirement for production of trophy bass: the lake must be stocked with rainbow trout.

In California, bass are classified as trophies, meaning more than 10 pounds, or super-trophies, meaning more than 15. Good fishing for trophies begins about 8 years after the initial stocking; for super-trophies, 12 years. Production of super-trophies drops off sharply as the word spreads and numbers of them are removed. Good reproduction and diminished fishing pressure, however, may result in another big-fish boom many years later.

Successful anglers pay close attention to big-bass cycles in different lakes. They also know the times of year when the fish are most vulnerable, exactly where to find them and the techniques most likely to entice them to bite.

In most of these lakes, threadfin shad are an important part of the forage base. The shad, which are pelagic, spend the summer cruising open water, usually in or above the thermocline. This means big bass are difficult to find and catch consistently in summer.

But the shad go deep in late fall and stay deep through winter. Small bass follow shad into the depths, but big ones seem reluctant to go deep. They're generally linked to some type of structure, usually at depths of 25 feet or less. Their locations are much more predictable, and because the bass are fattening up in preparation for spawning, they're feeding more heavily and are more willing to bite.

Once the shad move to deeper water, the predominant fall and winter big-bass foods are rainbow trout and crayfish, explaining why Folkestad's minnow-plug technique and Best's jigging technique are so effective.

Any type of hard-bottomed structure including long points, humps, rock bluffs, riprap banks, dug-out holes and old roadbeds may hold bass, if it has the right kind of bottom and deep water nearby. Bass will concentrate around something different on the structure, like a small rubble pile or an area of broken rock or brush.

Learning to quickly eliminate unproductive habitat and focus your efforts on prime water is a valuable skill no matter what you're fishing for. But it's especially important when you're looking for trophy fish, because there aren't many of them. It pays to have good electronics so you can pinpoint individual bass, schools of baitfish and key cover elements.

You may not be able to graph bass in the cool water because they tend to hug the bottom. But if you see anything that looks promising, work that depth thoroughly; big bass tend to be very depth-specific.

The bass feed most aggressively early and late in the day, but there's often a feeding peak in midday. Heavy boating and fishing activity usually slows the action, explaining why fishing tends to be better on weekdays than on weekends. Once the fish are disturbed, they move away from structure and don't feed.

When fishing pressure is heavy, it's important to get out early and stake out a spot. If you sleep in, you'll probably have to fish water that's already been combed by other anglers.

CALIFORNIA

Clear L.

Sacramento

L. Casitas

Castaic L.

L. Wohlford

L. Hodges

Los Angeles

Miramar Res.

San Vicente Res.

El Capitan Res.

Lower Otay Res.

San Diego

Barrett L.

L. Morena

California's Trophy Bass Program

Tagging studies enable biologists to check growth rates

The country's biggest largemouth swim in the man-made lakes that supply water to southern Californians. But these lakes have not always held such huge bass. The trophy bass program was born in 1959, when the San Diego County Fish and Game Commission stocked Florida-strain largemouth in Upper Otay Reservoir. Fish from that initial plant served as brood stock to supply Florida bass for many other California lakes.

The program has been incredibly successful, producing hundreds of largemouth over 14 pounds and seven over 20 since its inception. No other 20-pounders have been caught anywhere else in the world since 1932, when the current world-record bass, weighing 22.25 pounds, was caught in Montgomery Lake, Georgia. To date, the largest California bass weighed in at 22.01 pounds. It was taken in Castaic Lake in 1991. Most trophy bass enthusiasts agree it's only a matter of time before a California lake yields a new world record.

The reason California bass reach such mammoth size is explained by the following factors:

•During the coldwater months, the lakes are stocked with rainbow trout, which provide high-fat forage for fast growth. Most freshly stocked hatchery trout are about 9 to 11 inches long, just the right size for a good-sized bass to eat. They have little fear of predators, so they're easy for the bass to catch. These lakes also have healthy populations of crayfish and shad.

•The southern California climate allows a long growing season. The water temperature rarely drops below 50°F, so the fish grow all year long.

•The lakes producing the big bass have been stocked with the Florida-strain largemouth, whose inborn growth potential (table below) is considerably higher than that of the northern largemouth, the strain originally stocked in California. Not only does the Florida strain grow faster, they're more difficult to catch, so they tend to live longer.

Age and Growth of the 1961 Year Classes of Northern and Florida Largemouth Bass in El Capitan Reservoir, California

Northern Bass			Florida Bass		
AGE	LENGTH (IN.)	WEIGHT (LB.)	AGE	LENGTH (IN.)	WEIGHT (LB.)
1	6.07	.20	1	5.92	.15
2	11.62	1.10	2	12.75	1.50
3	14.73	2.15	3	15.69	2.84
4	16.37	2.91	4	17.65	4.15
5	17.94	3.80	5	20.39	6.44
6	19.11	4.57	6	22.05	8.32
7	20.28	5.39	7	23.08	9.61
8	20.35	5.53	8	23.36	10.05
9	no data	no data	9	24.80	12.15
10	no data	no data	10	25.63	13.32

Troy Folkestad's Minnow Plug Technique

"When the bass are zeroing in on stocked trout, it's tough to beat a big A.C.," says Troy Folkestad. These lures, originally designed to catch brown trout in lakes of California's High Sierra, have also drawn the attention of the state's trophy-bass fanatics.

"I was a doubter until I found one floating in Lake Castaic," Folkestad recalled. "But I tried it and started catching fish. I still have that plug – don't know exactly how many big bass I've caught on it, but it's a bunch.

"The fish home in on the A.C. because of its sound and vibration. It has a heavy, deep, thumping sound that trophy bass probably associate with big prey. An ordinary crankbait has a higher-pitched sound similar to that of smaller prey."

The name A.C. comes from the initials of the plug's inventor, Allan Cole. Made of cedar, the plug has a tapered face, rather than a lip, to make it dive. It will reach a depth of 5 feet on a cast, 15 feet when trolled. The jointed body, combined with a flexible rubber tail, produce a swimming action much like that of a rainbow trout.

Folkestad prefers the 9½- or 12-inch size in a rainbow trout color. But he feels the factory color is too vivid. "I like to drab it out a little so it looks more natural," he says.

Casting these big lures is easiest with a heavy flippin' stick. They work best when retrieved rapidly, so you'll need a high-speed reel. Set the drag tight, so it slips just a little on a hard hook set. Don't use mono heavier than 15-pound test, because it will cut down the lure's running depth. Check the line often for nicks or frays, and retie as needed.

"I like to fish this bait in the windiest, choppiest weather possible," Folkestad explained. "It disguises your approach, so you won't spook as many fish. And they don't get a good enough look at the plug to recognize it as a fake.

POPULAR big-bass plugs include the Arbogast A.C. Plug (main photo), the Thundertail (top in inset) and the Z-Plug (bottom in inset).

"I've found that moon phase is important, too. Over the years, 70 percent of my big bass have been caught within 4 days of the full moon.

"Another good time is right after they stock the trout. The big bass just move in and eat 'em. It's like cattle coming in to eat hay," Folkestad added. "The bass may hang around the trout-stocking area a few days, but then you'll have to look for them on their normal structure."

Folkestad fishes typical bass structure adjacent to deep water, such as flats, long points, isolated humps or any steep shoreline. But he focuses on very subtle, specific places with rocky or brushy cover, similar to the "rough spots" recommended by Randy Best. And like Best, Folkestad has found that bass in a specific piece of cover will strike only with a certain retrieve angle, so it pays to experiment.

Start fishing with the 12-inch A.C. and, using a sidearm lob cast, toss it as far as you can. This way, the plug can reach its maximum running depth to tempt less aggressive bass, and followers have more time to grab it.

Even in the cool water, a fast retrieve is usually best. Increase the speed even more when the plug bumps a rock or stick or you see a follower – this seems to trigger strikes. If a follower strikes short or doesn't strike at all, grab a rod rigged with a 9½-inch A.C. and cast well beyond the spot where you saw the fish.

Bass may smash the plug or just nip at it. If you think a bass has grabbed it, reel rapidly to tighten the line, then set the hook hard to drive in the thick trebles. With such a large plug, a big bass can easily shake the hook, especially if you let it reach the surface. If you see your line coming up, push your rod tip under to keep the fish down.

Folkestad prefers casting, but will troll with the plug when he thinks the bass are suspended off the structure over deep water. To get the plug to track deeper than 15 feet, switch to lead-core line.

"I'll do whatever it takes to catch fish," Folkestad said. "I've got nothing against live bait; in fact, it's pretty hard to top live crawdads. But I really like the challenge of trying to fool a big, wary bass on an artificial bait."

Folkestad's Plug-fishing Tips

TRY fishing any underwater extensions. Cast to the deep water and retrieve the plug along the extension into shallower water.

LOOK for small points along the bank, and cast beyond their tips. When you retrieve, the plug will bump the point, often triggering a strike.

WORK any shoreline where wave action has discolored the water. The dirty water makes it hard for a bass to distinguish the plug from a real trout.

Estimating Weight of a Trophy Bass

Measure girth with a flexible tape

If you want to release a trophy bass, but don't have an accurate scale, here's a handy formula that will give you a close approximation of its weight:

$$\frac{LENGTH \times LENGTH \times GIRTH}{1200} = WEIGHT$$

Length means total length in inches, from the tip of the jaw to the longest part of the tail. Girth is measured in inches around the thickest part of the body (left). The formula gives weight in pounds.

Here's an example of how it would work, assuming you've caught a 25-inch bass with a 20-inch girth:

$$\frac{25 \times 25 \times 20}{1200} = 10.42 \text{ POUNDS}$$

Randy Best's Jig-Fishing Technique

Equipment:

Rod: 6- to 6½-foot, medium-heavy, fast-action, high-sensitivity graphite baitcaster
Reel: baitcaster
Line: 8- to 10- pound low-vis mono in clear water; 10- to 12-pound in slightly off-color water
Lure: ¼- to ½-ounce football jig

"Prime time for jiggin' is when the bass are holding tight to cover and chewin' on crawdads," Best contends. "They're a lot easier to locate than when they're chasing shad in open water."

Best prefers a football-head jig (left and below), because it can be retrieved with a slow, tantalizing action, which he believes mimics that of a crayfish rearing up to assume a defensive posture. At rest, it lies flat on the bottom, but when you pull on it, the head pivots downward and the tail rises. A football-head also sinks vertically, rather than gliding away from cover like some other types of jigs.

Football jigs have a unique rocking action

Always be on the alert for boulders, rock piles, brush clumps or any "rough spots," areas of rocky or gravelly bottom that seem to grab the lure during the retrieve. "If you don't feel something dif-

FOOTBALL JIGS used by Best include (1) rubber-legged jig with size 11 pork frog, which has a large profile that appeals to aggressive bass; (2) vinyl-skirted jig with twin-tail, which has a smaller profile better for finicky bass; (3) hair jig with twin-tail and brushguard, good for finicky bass in brushy cover.

ferent, you're not in big-bass water," Best says.

Cast the jig well past likely cover, then feed line as it sinks to the bottom. Work it through the cover zone with a slow, methodical retrieve, pulling it along the bottom a few inches at a time. Try to maintain constant bottom contact rather than hopping the jig.

Boat control is critical. It's usually best to work the jig from shallow to deep, mainly because you won't snag up as much as you would the opposite way. But there are times when other angles work better. If a bass is lying in a rock crevice, for instance, you may have to cast from a very specific angle to put the lure where it will be seen. And if the fish won't strike on a downhill retrieve, try an uphill.

Don't expect a crushing strike. Sometimes a big bass just closes its mouth on the bait and you feel a little extra weight. Other times, you feel a sharp tap, meaning that the bass has inhaled the bait.

You may not get a lot of hits, so what you do after feeling a strike is crucial. Because you're making such long casts, line stretch makes it difficult to set the hook. Set with a strong wrist snap, keeping your elbows against your body for maximum leverage and control. Then quickly crank down and set again to be sure the barb is sunk.

Most of these lakes have few obstacles, so once you hook a fish, you don't have to horse it in. Let it tire in deep water; this way, it's less likely to jump and throw the hook.

"I'd rather jig for big bass than throw giant plugs at 'em," says Best. "You got to remember, a lot of those big fish are just plain lazy. They'd rather sit on a rock pile and root out crawdads than chase a trout. Those are the fish that are going to attack a slowly crawling jig."

Football-jigging Tips

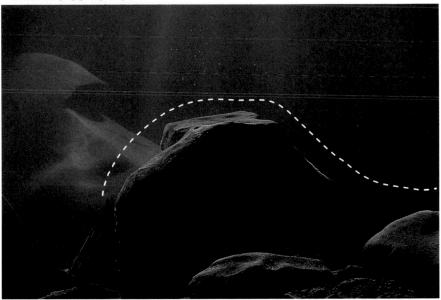

RETRIEVE a football jig slowly, with no sharp twitches, so it stays in contact with the bottom (dotted line). If you work it too fast, it will ride above bass tucked into crevices in the cover.

SOFTEN your pork trailers so they have more action by placing them in a rock tumbler, along with some marble-size rocks and water, and tumbling them overnight. If desired, custom-dye the pork at the same time by adding dye.

SLICE your pork trailer as shown to give it more flexibility and extra action. Make about three slices down to the skin.

MAKE a lively twin-tail from a floating worm. Slice it lengthwise, then melt a small wedge of the plastic into the V to keep the tails apart.

85

Advanced Spinnerbait Techniques

Blades 'N Grubs:
The Right Combination for Muddy-Water Bass

Optimal Conditions:

Type of Water: any reservoir that muddies up after a heavy rain
Season: pre-spawn
Water Temperature: inflow temperature warmer than main lake
Weather: warm, sunny
Water Stage: high
Water Depth: 10 feet or less
Water Clarity: beginning to clear after being muddy
Time of Day: afternoon and evening

Heavy rains in late winter and early spring mean big trouble for many anglers on normally clear reservoirs. Huge quantities of silt flushed in from the main river and from tributaries muddy up the entire lake, with the possible exception of the extreme lower end, where silt has had more time to settle out.

Creeks swollen by early season rain pour into upper ends of creek arms at a time when they're holding lots of pre-spawn bass. The bass don't leave, even when water clarity is reduced to a few inches, but they can be very difficult to catch.

Greg Hines, who spends a good deal of time fishing Arizona's Lake Roosevelt, doesn't even try to catch these muddy-water bass. "It's too tough when every creek is belching out water that looks like heavily creamed coffee," he says. "The secret is to find the creeks that clear quickest. The fish there are much more cooperative."

Some bass permanently reside in these creek arms, and a gully-washer that muddies the water makes fishing tough – anytime. So the idea of looking for the fastest-clearing creeks applies at other times of the year, as well.

Hines, a former winner of the U.S. Open and U.S. Bass World Championship, has devised a method for quickly finding and catching bass around these clear creeks. When he locates a creek that he feels is clear enough, he quickly scours the area with a spinnerbait, hoping to find active fish. If he gets enough action, he sticks with the spinnerbait. Otherwise, he switches to a slower presentation, using a Texas-rigged grub to coax strikes from less-aggressive fish in heavier cover.

"It's a tough combination to beat," Hines contends. "One method or the other will usually do the job. If it doesn't, you're just not going to catch them – period."

Greg Hines

Hometown:
Gilbert, Arizona
Favorite Waters for Technique:
Lakes Roosevelt and San Carlos, Arizona
Career Highlights:
Winner: 1981 U.S. Open on Lake Mead, Nevada; 1986 U.S. Bass World Championship on Lake Tawakoni, Texas

When and Where to Find Pre-Spawn Bass in Muddied Reservoirs

Differences in the watersheds of different tributaries determine which ones clear first and begin to draw bass. A creek flowing through a rocky gorge, for instance, clears much sooner than one draining highly erodible agricultural lands. And creeks draining small watersheds tend to clear sooner than those draining large ones.

In spring, a creek's water temperature is also important. If the inflow is warmer than the water in the rest of the creek arm, baitfish (particularly shad) will congregate around the inflow area and attract bass. If there are shad around, you'll see lots of bird activity. Creeks fed by snowmelt at high altitudes, or those draining deep, shaded valleys run colder than creeks that are fed by rainfall and drain open terrain at low elevations.

Let's assume there are two creeks that both have the right makeup to draw bass. The larger one will draw the most fish, simply because it influences a larger portion of the reservoir. And a creek arm with a well-defined channel leading from the back end out to the mouth will probably draw more bass than one with a flat basin. The channel serves as a roadway for bass moving up the creek arm, and once the water starts to fall, it offers a deeper-water retreat.

Changes in water level further complicate the bass-location puzzle (below). If the level remains stable as the creek is clearing, bass move into flooded brush in the extreme back ends of the creek arms. You'll normally find them at depths of three feet or less, holding tight to the cover. But the pattern changes when the level is falling, as it normally is when the water starts to clear. Instead of holding tight to the cover, they pull away from the bank and seek steeper structure, such as a definite creek channel. Or they may suspend over the first significant break out from shore. Instinct tells the bass to pull away from the bank when the water level is falling; otherwise, they could become stranded in an isolated pocket with no escape route to open water.

Although bass continue to feed when the water level is falling, fishing is not as good as when the level is stable. The bass are cruising about much more and are not as predictable.

Rising- vs. Falling-water Bass Location

Rising water draws bass (red) tight into shallow, newly flooded cover; falling water pushes the fish (blue) out to the first break

HINES' FAVORITE SPINNERBAITS include (1) ½-ounce willow-leaf, such as the Classic Hart Throb, for working the bottoms of bushes; (2) ½-ounce Colorado, such as the Hart Throb I, for slow-rolling in cold water; (3) ¼-ounce tandem willow-leaf, such as the Hart Throb II, for maximum lift when bass are high in the bushes.

Spinnerbait Techniques

Once you find a likely looking creek, start fishing with a spinnerbait. "It's a great search bait, especially in discolored water," Hines says. "And it's versatile. It lets you quickly scout an area to find fish, yet you can slow-roll it over stick-ups or brush piles, helicopter it alongside a submerged stump or work it at a controlled depth to catch bass suspended over a creek-channel break."

Spinnerbait selection depends on the mood of the bass and their position in the cover. When they're inactive, as they often are in the morning before the water has warmed, they ride low in the cover. That's the time for slowly retrieving a deep-running spinnerbait, about ½ ounce, with a single willow-leaf blade. But if the water is below 50°F, a bait with a single Colorado blade is a better choice, because it turns more easily with an ultraslow retrieve. When the afternoon sun has warmed the water and activated the bass, try a lighter, high-riding model, such as a ¼-ounce tandem-spin, retrieved at moderate speed.

Equipment:
Rod: 6½-foot medium-heavy, fast-action graphite baitcaster
Reel: medium-speed baitcaster
Line: 14- to 17-pound mono
Lure: ¼- to ½-ounce spinnerbait

To maximize the amount of water covered, move rapidly with your troll motor. How you work the cover depends mainly on the water level. When the water is stable, for instance, bass usually hold tight to woody cover on flats adjacent to the creek channel. Make short casts to specific objects and be sure to work the thickest part of the cover. If your casts are too long, a hooked fish could easily wrap itself in the tangle. When the water is falling, bass often suspend over or near the creek channel break, still relating to cover, but not as close to it. Then, make longer casts to cover more water and get the bait a little deeper.

Pay close attention to the way the bass strike. An active fish hits hard enough to throw slack into your line. A sluggish one just feels like extra weight. When you hook a fish, keep firm, steady pressure on it, letting the rod act as a shock absorber. Try to direct it away from the cover. You'll lose too many fish if you try to rip them through it.

How to Add Flash to a Spinnerbait Skirt

REMOVE the skirt from a spinnerbait, open the O-ring with a longnose pliers and insert several strands of Mylar or Flashabou (left). Trim them to the same length as the skirt, then replace the skirt. Flash from the reflective strips increases the bait's visibility (right), a big advantage in low-clarity water.

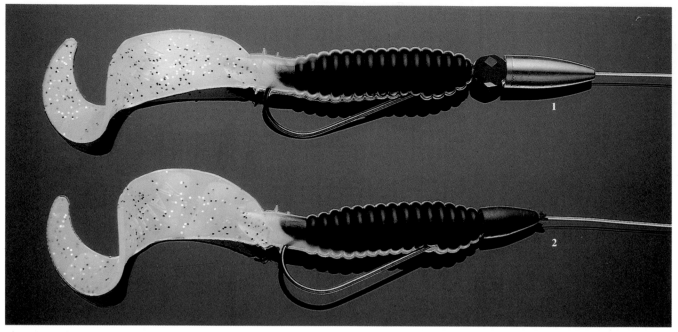

GRUB-RIGGING OPTIONS include (1) curlytail, such as Kalin's K3 Triple Threat, Texas-rigged with ⅛-ounce brass sinker and polished glass bead, for maximum noise

when shaking; (2) same bait, rigged Texas-style with ⅛-ounce bullet sinker pegged in place with rubber strands (opposite), for penetrating thick cover.

Grub-Fishing Techniques

Rig the grub with a size ³⁄₀ straight-shank worm hook and a ⅛-ounce bullet sinker. Many anglers add a glass bead between the hook and sinker for extra noise. Flip or pitch the bait into visible cover, such as flooded brush, keeping your casts short.

Because you're so close to the fish, it's important to keep boat noise to a minimum. "Instead of constantly changing speeds with your trolling motor, try to keep it on a steady speed," Hines advises. "This way, there's less creaking and squeaking from the bracket, and the fish aren't as likely to spook from the changing rhythm of the prop."

After flipping the grub, vertically jig it in place, using a branch as a fulcrum (opposite). Shake the grub occasionally for a different look. If the water is falling, try slow-swimming the grub through sparser cover close to the creek-channel break. With so little line out, strikes should be easy to feel.

Set the hook with a sharp wrist snap powerful enough to drive the hook through the grub and into the bass's jaw. Then try to pull the fish away from the cover before it has a chance to tangle. The long, medium-power rod and narrow-spool reel match up well with the light grub, and the rod flexes enough on the hook set to prevent breaking the line.

"When the water gets muddy in early spring, most fishermen throw in the towel," Hines observed. "But I see it as an opportunity. I've got a lot less water to cover, and with this combination, I can usually coax some fish to bite."

Equipment:

Rod: 7½-foot, medium-power, fast-action graphite flippin' stick
Reel: narrow-spool baitcaster
Line: 15-pound low-vis mono
Lure: ⅛-ounce Texas-rigged curlytail grub

If you think the bass are around, but they won't hit a spinnerbait, try a slower presentation using a 5-inch Texas-rigged curlytail grub. "A curlytail draws more strikes than other soft plastics in the dingy water," Hines insists, "because its wide tail creates tremendous vibration, even with a slow retrieve."

A grub is generally a better producer at water temperatures less than 50°F, when the fish aren't "chasing." But grubs sometimes outproduce other baits even at warmer temperatures. So whenever you finish working an area with a spinnerbait, always go back through with a grub.

How to Fish a Grub

FLIP OR PITCH just beyond a bush, then swim your grub toward it until you feel it contact a branch.

HOOK your line over an exposed branch, shaking it at different depths to find the bass. Work the bush thoroughly, then flip to another.

How to Peg a Sinker with Strands from a Spinnerbait Skirt

PUSH a needle threader through the nose of a bullet sinker threaded onto your line. Insert living-rubber strands into the threader.

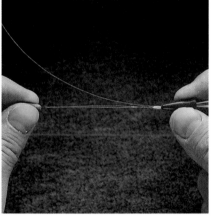

PULL the rubber strands into the hole in the sinker to secure it on the line.

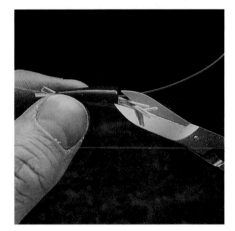

TRIM the excess rubber. Because the sinker cannot slide away, it will carry the grub down into the cover.

Bass-location Tips

NOTE the precise location of exposed structure, such as a rock pile, when the water is low. Then, when the structure is submerged, you'll know right where to fish.

LOOK for fish-eating birds, such as grebes and gulls, around the mouth of a tributary. The birds are drawn by baitfish, which also draw bass.

Spinnerbaiting the Wood: Ken Cook's Strategy

Optimal Conditions:

Type of Water: relatively new reservoirs with lots of timber and brush

Season: pre- and post-spawn

Water Temperature: at least 50°F

Weather: overcast

Water Stage: stable

Water Depth: less than 12 feet

Water Clarity: less than 3 feet

Time of Day: warm mornings; late in the day

Known as one of pro bass fishing's top "blade men," Ken Cook relies on spinnerbaits in a wide variety of bass-fishing situations. "Spinnerbaits are like crescent wrenches," he observed. "You can adjust them to suit lots of different conditions."

But Cook's favorite place to use spinnerbaits is in shallow timber and brush. He knows he can put the bait where the fish are and draw strikes with little risk of snagging. This method works best in spring, when spawning bass move into creek arms with plenty of woody cover, but it can also be effective in fall, when bass follow shad migrations back into the creek arms.

"The sound of a spinnerbait triggers reflex strikes," Cook says, "and in profile, it looks like a shad. But don't give the bass credit for thinking it's anything. They hit it because of its abnormal vibrations."

Cook considers spinnerbaits "high-percentage" lures. It's tough for bass to shake the big single hook, so you don't lose many of them. "Some days, I catch every one that hits."

An 11-time BASS Masters Classic qualifier, Cook has found blades to be highly profitable on the professional bass-fishing trail. Most notable of his numerous tournament wins was the 1991 BASS Masters Classic, held on Chesapeake Bay.

Ken Cook

Hometown:
Meers, Oklahoma

Favorite Waters for Technique:
Buggs Island Lake, Virginia/N. Carolina; Ray Roberts Lake, Texas; Lake Eufala, Oklahoma

Career Highlights:
Winner: 1983 Missouri BASSMASTER Invitational; 1983 SUPER B.A.S.S. Tournament; 1985 U.S. Bass World Championship; 1987 New York BASSMASTER Invitational: 1991 BASS Masters Classic
Qualified for BASS Masters Classic 11 times

When and Where to Fish Spinnerbaits in Woody Cover

Cook starts using spinnerbaits during the pre-spawn period, as soon as the water temperature tops the 50-degree mark and the bass are feeding actively. But when they're actually spawning, he prefers a slower bait. "I like something that stays in their face for a longer time," he says. His usual choices are a tube jig, minnow plug, weightless lizard, or soft stickbait. He goes back to a spinnerbait after the fish have completed spawning.

You can catch bass on a spinnerbait all day and under any weather conditions, but you'll have to fish tighter to the cover in high sun. Early and late in the day or under cloudy skies, the fish roam more and may be shallower.

Spinnerbaits are an excellent choice in water of lower-than-normal clarity, where sound plays an important role. They excel in newer reservoirs with lots of standing timber, but they're also effective in older reservoirs with many fallen trees and in rivers or reservoirs with an abundance of stumps and brush.

Creek arms with a deep, well-defined creek channel hold lots of bass from the pre-spawn through the post-spawn period, and again in fall, when they're following the shad. The best arms have a line of standing timber adjacent to the deep water and a firm bottom for spawning. Other bass hangouts in good creek arms include ditches along old road beds, fencelines bordering old fields, or any kind of tree row.

Another consideration in selecting a good creek arm is water clarity. Creeks arms that are permanently discolored make prime fishing areas. But those that are temporarily discolored due to heavy runoff are seldom productive. The sudden drop in clarity evidently causes the fish to stop feeding.

Early in the pre-spawn, you'll find the most bass near the mouths of creek arms. But as the water warms and spawning time approaches, they move farther into the arms, eventually settling into the back ends of secondary creek arms and coves that receive lots of sunlight and warm early. After spawning, the fish hold in deeper water just outside these bedding areas, gradually working their way toward the main lake.

Remember, not all bass are in the same stage of spawning or in the same areas at the same time. As a rule, creek arms at the upper end of a reservoir warm earliest and draw the first spawners.

Where to Use Spinnerbaits in Older Reservoirs

STUMP FIELDS. In many cases, trees were cut before the reservoir filled, leaving large stump fields. In others, the treetops rotted off. The stumps make ideal bass cover, especially if they're near deep water, and are sometimes used as spawning substrate.

FALLEN TREES. Shoreline erosion and wind cause trees to topple into the water. The best ones are those that fall in along steep banks, where a creek channel abuts the shore. You may find bass in the treetops, or in shallower water near the trunk.

FLOODED BRUSH. A major cover type in most rivers and reservoirs, brush and small trees develop along shorelines and on humps during low water. When flooded, they draw bass that normally hold in deeper water, where they are difficult to find.

OLD FENCEROWS are often the only cover remaining on flooded farm fields. Bass are more likely to follow the fencerows in their daily movements than roam over featureless flats.

STOCK TANKS draw bass because of the flooded trees, deep water and firm bottom on the dikes.

FIRM-BOTTOM AREAS draw spawning bass and often hold good numbers of fish later in the season, as well.

OLD CREEK CHANNELS make ideal bass habitat because of the deep water adjacent to rows of cover.

OLD ROADBEDS draw bass because of their firm surface and adjacent deep water in the ditches.

How to Spinnerbait the Wood

A spinnerbait simplifies the job of finding fish in timber and brush, because you can work the cover quickly. But your spinnerbait must suit the type of water and cover you're fishing.

Cook prefers single-spins most of the time because they make the most vibration and are best suited for a stop-and-go retrieve. But when fishing over shallow weeds or in clear water, he often switches to a tandem-spin. It has more lift, and the counter-rotating blades dampen the vibration, for a more subtle presentation. Here are some other considerations:

•Weight. The head must be heavy enough to offset the torque of the blade. If the head is too light for the blade, the whole lure will spin or track through the water in a tilted position (below). Cook uses a ½-ounce spinnerbait most of the time, although he goes to a ¼-ounce in very shallow water and a ¾-ounce in deep water. Wind, current or deep water require a heavier-than-normal spinnerbait.

Looking down at a properly balanced spinnerbait (top) vs. one with a head that's too light (bottom)

•Blade size. A big blade has more lift, so it is a good choice for shallow presentations and, because it makes more vibration, is effective in muddy water. But a bigger blade also has more torque. If you switch blades, be sure you don't throw the bait out of balance. You can switch to a smaller blade, which is a good option in clear water or when you want the bait to run deeper, without affecting the balance. When bass are feeding on shad, choose a blade about the same size as a shad's body.

•Blade style. A willow-leaf blade is the best choice for fishing in clear water, and tends to shed weeds better than other blade styles. Because it produces the least vibration, your presentation will be more natural. A Colorado blade generates more vibration, so it's best in murky water. It's also the most effective for helicoptering, and because it has more lift, it works well for fishing over weedtops.

•Head shape. In woody cover, use a wide head; it helps deflect branches from the hook and tends to ride up in the "Y" of a branch. But if the head is too wide, it may wedge rather than ride up. A narrow, cone-shaped head is a better choice in heavy weeds.

•Color. Cook's favorite all-around color pattern includes a metal-flake skirt with a combination of white and blue for a natural look, along with chartreuse for visibility. It has a white head with a red cheek and big eyes, and a gold blade. In very clear water, he makes a minor adjustment, switching to a skirt in which the white strands have red, instead of gold, flakes. "Combination colors are more efficient because of the contrast and natural look," he says.

Cook seldom uses a spinnerbait without a plastic trailer, preferably one made of harder-than-normal plastic so it doesn't slip off the collar. He favors white or pearl-white for most conditions; chartreuse-pearl for extra visibility in muddy water. The trailer not only adds color and wiggle, it provides bulk, which Cook believes makes it easier for fish to inhale the bait. "A bulky trailer decreases the number of missed strikes because it gives them something to suck in," he contends.

When beginning your search for bass, move the boat faster than normal and cast only to the targets that seem most likely to hold fish. When you get a strike, slow down and work the area more thoroughly, casting to all likely targets.

As you fish, a locational pattern is apt to emerge; you're catching bass only on the shady side of big trees near the creek channel, or around brush piles on shallow flats. As the pattern becomes more definite, you can increase your efficiency by keying on a particular cover type.

Spinnerbait-Casting Techniques

Casting accuracy and versatility are crucial when fishing woody cover. It may be necessary to place the bait in a pocket no more than a few inches in diameter, or cast beneath a limb only inches above the water. If you're not proficient with the casting techniques shown below, you'll spend most of your time untangling baits from branches.

BOLO CAST. From a forehand or backhand position with the rod tip low, use a short, circular wrist motion to whip the bait around the rod tip (arrow). The lure travels in a low trajectory and makes little splash. This is the best technique when branches restrict your casting motion.

PITCHIN'. With the lure in your free hand and the rod angled slightly downward (top), sweep the rod in a short upward arc so the lure travels in a low trajectory (bottom). This cast is very accurate, gets your lure under low branches, and creates minimal splash.

FOREHAND. When there is an open casting lane and no branches to restrict rod movement on your forehand side, cast with a sweeping sidearm motion. The lure will splash down hard; cast well past the spot to avoid spooking fish. This technique gives good distance, but is not recommended for precise accuracy or a low trajectory.

BACKHAND. Used for much the same purposes as forehand casting, this technique works well where there is an open casting lane and no branches to restrict rod movement on your backhand side. As in forehand casting, be sure to cast well past your target so the splashdown doesn't scare the fish.

Cook's Favorite Spinnerbait Retrieves

There's really no right or wrong way to work a spinnerbait; it will catch fish on a wide variety of retrieves. Cook puts it like this: "If your spinnerbait is wet, you can catch a fish on it."

But more often than not, bass prefer a specific type of retrieve. You must experiment to find the proper speed, depth and tempo, or you risk fishing through bass that may respond to a different retrieve variation. The types of retrieves Cook uses most often are shown on these pages.

"It's important to be in contact with the blade (feel it thumping) at all times to detect strikes," says Cook. "If you feel the blade stop turning, set the hook."

His advice for landing bass in heavy timber: "Use big line and pull hard." He recommends a powerful 6½- to 7-foot, long-handled rod and a heavy-duty reel whose gears won't strip when horsing out a fish. The reel should have a reliable drag that won't "freeze up" when set just below the breaking point of the line.

When you hook a fish, keep its head up so it can't dive and tangle around a branch. If a fish does wrap you up, don't try to rip it out. Use your troll motor, go to the fish and try to unwrap it. "It's fishermen, not fish, that break the line," Cook contends.

For Ken Cook, spinnerbaiting in timber and brush is the most enjoyable form of bass fishing. "It's why I got hooked on bass fishing years ago," he mused. "You're working heavy cover, getting aggressive strikes and catching quality fish."

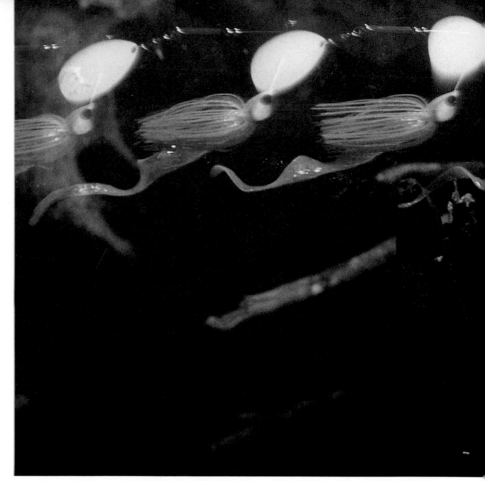

STOP-AND-GO. Just as a bass is more likely to grab an injured baitfish than one swimming normally, it's more likely to hit an erratically moving bait. Cook uses some sort of stop-and-go retrieve 90 percent of the time because it is more likely

HELICOPTERING. This retrieve, an extreme variation of the stop-and-go, is most effective when fish are holding at the base of cover or feeding on the bottom. When your bait comes to a target that could hold fish, stop reeling; the blade will spin as the bait sinks, and that's when fish usually hit. The silt kicked up when the bait hits bottom also helps trigger strikes.

to draw a reflex strike. Experiment with different stop-and-go tempos to find the combination largemouth prefer on a given day. A stop-and-go retrieve is ideal for fishing around woody cover. You can bump the bait off the wood, allow it to flutter a little, then resume your retrieve, drawing the attention of any bass using the cover.

BULGING. This retrieve draws explosive surface strikes, especially when the water temperature exceeds 60°F and the surface is glassy calm. Keep your rod tip high and reel fast enough so the blade almost, but not quite, breaks the surface.

SHAKING. When there is no visible cover, such as a stump or stick-up, to deflect the bait and give it an erratic action, shake the rod tip rapidly as you reel. You don't need to shake as much in heavy timber or brush; the bait gets action from bouncing off the branches.

Tips for Catching Short Strikers

For spinnerbait fishermen, short strikes are a common problem. If the fish are consistently nudging the bait but you're not hooking them, or you're losing too many hooked fish, you'll have to make some adjustments.

You could solve the problem by slipping on a long-shank trailer hook over the main hook, but the trailer would snag up too much in woody cover. Here are some of Cook's suggestions for improving your hooking percentage.

SHORTEN the skirt or thin it out so the bait has a smaller profile. This way, a bass is more likely to grab the hook.

SWITCH blades to downsize the bait. If the blade is attached with a split ring, open it with a split-ring pliers.

CHANGE the color of the skirt or trailer to draw more aggressive strikes.

SHORTEN the trailer if you feel bass are nipping at the tail and missing the hook.

The Boom-Bust Phenomenon

Ever wonder why new reservoirs provide such fantastic fishing in their first few years of life? Or why fishing in old ones is not so good?

As a reservoir fills, trees, brush and other terrestrial vegetation is flooded and soon dies. The nutrients released by decomposition of this organic matter and leaching from the soil trigger an explosion of plankton and bottom organisms, fueling a concurrent rise in the baitfish population. The rising water also kills a tremendous quantity of terrestrial animals, such as worms, slugs and insects, providing instant fish food. With such a profusion of food and an abundance of flooded timber and brush for cover, high growth and survival rates produce a gamefish "boom."

Another reason for the boom is the open *niche* created by the rising water. Although some fish were present in the river before it was impounded, or in farm ponds within the reservoir basin, the water is relatively empty. With few large predator fish, the survival rate of stocked fish and naturally produced fry is much higher than in an older lake.

But as the decomposition and leaching processes wind down, cover disappears and predators become established, the picture changes. There are fewer nutrients to produce the plankton needed to keep baitfish populations high, more predators to eat the baitfish and young gamefish and less cover to protect them. In addition, siltation covers spawning areas and reduces production of bottom organisms needed by gamefish and baitfish. As gamefish populations wane, rough fish start to take over.

The duration of the boom period is highly variable, ranging from as little as 3 to as much as 20 years, depending mainly on the amount of terrestrial vegetation present when the reservoir starts to fill, and the rate of filling. A slow fill rate may extend nutrient release over several years, and the new vegetation flooded each year makes good spawning habitat.

When the "bust" begins, often only a few years after the boom's peak, the sportfishing catch diminishes to one-third or less of that during the boom and stays that way for the remainder of the reservoir's life. Some reservoirs, however, have been rejuvenated when aquatic plants, such as milfoil and hydrilla, became established. The plants provide habitat for young gamefish and food organisms, and add to the water fertility when they decompose.

The graph that follows, based on data collected on Beaver Lake, Arkansas (filled in 1963), depicts a typical boom-bust scenario. The bass-population bust, which began in 1971, was followed by a carp-population boom, beginning in 1972.

Changes in Populations of Largemouth Bass and Carp in Beaver Lake, Arkansas — 1963-79

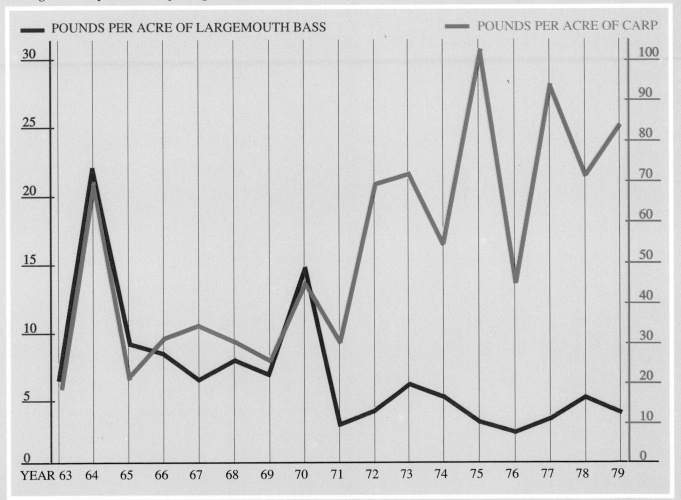

Calling Up Clearwater Smallmouth

Optimal Conditions:
Type of Water: ultraclear lakes
Season: summer and fall
Water Temperature: 50°F or higher
Weather: windy or rainy
Water Stage: any stage
Water Depth: as deep as 40 feet
Water Clarity: at least 10 feet
Time of Day: anytime, if weather is favorable

Ask most any smallmouth expert to outline his strategy for catching the fish in ultraclear lakes, and here's what he's likely to say:

- use smaller-than-normal baits
- select natural or drab colors
- use lighter-than-normal line
- fish deep

But Rick Lillegard, a veteran guide and tournament angler from Atkinson, New Hampshire, doesn't always heed this standard advice. In fact, a technique he uses in Lake Winnipesaukee violates every one of the usual clearwater smallmouth rules. "It may sound crazy," he says, "but it puts a lot of fish in the boat in a hurry and allows me to cover a lot of water."

Pioneered in the early 80s by Keith Kline of the Fleck Lure Company and Danny Correia, a B.A.S.S. touring pro, the technique involves "calling up" smallmouth over water as deep as 40 feet by retrieving big, often bright-colored, spinnerbaits just beneath the surface. "It's becoming more popular," says Lillegard, "but it doesn't seem logical to most people, so they won't even try it."

Some top pros, however, have been trying it. Rick Clunn used big spinnerbaits to call up enough smallmouth to win the 1992 New York BASSMASTER Invitational on Lake Ontario. And the technique has become one of the favorites of 1992 B.A.S.S. Angler of the Year, Kevin Van Dam, who routinely uses it to catch smallmouth in clear Michigan lakes.

Clearwater smallmouth often pursue suspended forage in open water, and this technique takes advantage of that behavior. Lillegard knows the bass are suspended, because they often grab the bait as soon as it hits the water. The main reason the technique works so well is that it doesn't require a pinpoint presentation; all you have to do is cast over an area known to hold fish, and they'll come up for the bait.

Rick Lillegard

Hometown:
Atkinson, New Hampshire
Favorite Waters for Technique:
Winnipesaukee, Squam and Sunapee lakes, New Hampshire
Career Highlights:
1989 and 1991 Angler of the Year, North American Bass Assn. Team Trail; 1992 American Bass Assn. Team Champion

When and Where to Call Up Smallmouth

You can call up smallmouth over deep water in most any clear lake, but the technique works best in those with high smallmouth populations and pelagic baitfish that roam open water in large schools.

In the Northeast, for instance, smallmouth have plenty of pelagic forage in the form of smelt and small white perch, which scour open water for zooplankton and small minnows. The bass also eat yellow perch, which have pelagic tendencies in these lakes. In clear Canadian-shield lakes, smallmouth patrol open water to find ciscoes.

The technique is effective in waters of this type because smallmouth that feed on pelagic baitfish tend to be highly aggressive and willing to chase baits they've spotted from a considerable distance.

Evidence that open-water smallmouth eat yellow perch

Best Places to Call Up Clearwater Smallmouth

NARROWS. A narrows may be a channel between two islands, an island and shore, or two basins of a lake. Current induced by the wind funneling water through a narrows draws baitfish and smallmouth.

SADDLES. These subsurface connectors link two pieces of structure, such as two humps, or an island and shore. They serve as underwater highways for bass moving between structures.

BIG BOULDERS. Boulders the size of a car, or even larger, make prime year-round smallmouth cover. The best boulders lie on a break between shallow and deep water. Look for fish along the shady side.

SUNKEN ISLANDS. Large sunken islands that top out at 10 feet or less, with a clean, sand-boulder bottom, irregular shape and variable depth, make excellent summertime smallmouth habitat.

After smallmouth finish spawning, look for them around big boulders or beds of cabbage or sandgrass just outside the shoal areas where they spawned. Others lie suspended in open water, but still relating to the breakline or deeper sandgrass beds. Once the fish set up in these locations, they'll remain there until cooling water drives them deeper in mid-fall and makes them less aggressive.

Lillegard has his best success calling up bass relating to points and weed flats connected to shoreline breaks, but it's also possible to call up bass relating to isolated structure, such as a sunken island.

As summer progresses, young pelagic baitfish grow large enough to interest smallmouth and draw them from the breakline. The bass spend more and more of their time relating to deep water, either holding on the bottom or suspending. But some smallmouth remain on points and weed flats until mid-fall.

In shield lakes or other clear waters with a lot of exposed bedrock, smallmouth are strongly drawn to sandy structure, because it offers the only available weed growth. You'll find the fish on sandy humps and points, along sandy shoreline breaks, and even in sandy bays. An exposed sandy shoreline provides a visual clue on where you're likely to find sandy structure in the lake.

Calling up smallmouth is easiest in windy weather. "Get out where there's wave action," Lillegard advises. "It's easier to fish the calm water, but you'll catch more fish along the windy shores." Another good time for calling them up is in rainy weather; raindrops break up the calm surface.

SANDY SHORELINES. Good smallmouth weeds, such as sandgrass and cabbage (right), grow on sandy bottoms. A sandy shoreline is a good indicator of a sandy, weedy bottom farther out from shore.

WEEDY FLATS. Sandgrass (left), a short, stringy weed that grows in water as deep as 25 feet, is a smallmouth magnet from spring through fall. Cabbage (right) does not grow as deep, but is equally attractive to the fish.

SPAWNING FLATS. Large, shallow flats with a sand-rock bottom are hubs of early season smallmouth activity. Try the top of the flat when they're spawning; otherwise, you'll find them where the flat slopes into deep water.

EXTENDED LIPS. Look for smallmouth around the ends of underwater extensions of major points from early summer through fall. In many lakes, these extensions are easy to find because of buoys (arrow) at their tips.

How to Call Up Clearwater Smallmouth

Equipment:
Rod: long-handled, 6½- to 7½-foot, medium-heavy- to heavy-power, fast-action, graphite baitcaster
Reel: high-speed baitcaster
Line: 14- to 17-pound-test, low-visibility mono
Lure: ¾- to 1-ounce tandem Colorado-blade spinnerbait tipped with curlytail grub

A smallmouth that will charge to the surface from deep water to grab a bait is obviously in a highly aggressive mood. As Lillegard puts it, "These fish are really supercharged and bustin', so you don't have to put the bait in their face and you don't have to tease them into hitting it.

"You know when you're bit – it's a solid reflex strike. They try to tear the blades off the bait. Lots of times, they're on it just as it hits the water."

This level of aggression means you can work a likely spot very quickly. If the fish are going to bite, they'll bite right away, so the idea is to move rapidly and keep hitting new water.

Lillegard's usual strategy is first casting to visible shallow-water cover, such as boulders and weed patches, then casting over the deep water adjacent to them. Simply cast a big, tandem-blade spinnerbait as far from the boat as you can and retrieve rapidly so it tracks about a foot or so beneath the surface. Long casts not only increase your coverage, they allow you to reach smallmouth that haven't been spooked by the boat.

You'll need a long, powerful rod for distance casting with such a heavy, wind-resistant bait. For two-handed power casting, choose a rod with an extra-long handle. A 6½-foot rod is adequate most of the time, but in a strong wind a 7½-footer works better. It helps you punch your casts into the wind, and quickly take up slack for strong hook sets. A high-

LILLEGARD'S FAVORITE BAITS for calling up smallmouth include (1) tandem Colorado-blade spinnerbait, such as a Hog Sticker, with size 7 to 8 rear blade and size 3 to 4 front blade. Add a size 2/0 to 3/0 trailer hook tipped with a 3- to 5-inch grub as shown; (2) stickbait, such as a Zara Spook, about 4½ inches long; (3) floating minnow plug, such as a Bomber Long A (model 15A).

108

speed reel starts the bait moving before it can sink, and keeps it riding high in the water.

Despite the clear water, Lillegard normally uses bright colors. "Seems like high visibility is the key," he theorizes. "I use an all-chartreuse spinnerbait most of the time, but when it's calm and sunny, I may go with a white body and nickel blades."

If the water is calm and spinnerbaits aren't working as well as you'd like, try a stickbait, such as a Zara Spook. Under low-light conditions, use a black one; other times, a minnow or frog pattern. A good-sized bait, about 4½ inches long, works well for big bass, but when the fish are fussy, you may do better with a 3-incher.

Cast the bait as far as you can, let it rest motionless for 30 seconds or so, then walk it from side to side

(p. 110). After retrieving about 15 feet, reel in and make another cast. The fish usually strike while the bait is at rest or just after you start to reel.

Another option is a floating minnow plug. Lillegard prefers a gold or silver plug with a green back. On a rippled surface, retrieve with rapid sharp jerks to give the plug an erratic action. When the surface is calm, let the plug rest for a few seconds, nudge it a few times (p. 110), then switch to the fast, jerky retrieve. With minnow plugs and stickbaits, use light line, about 10-pound test; heavy line may spook fish in the clear water.

"I don't know of any other technique as exciting as calling up smallmouth," says Lillegard. "When a bass spots your bait, he doesn't want to eat it, he wants to kill it – that's why I love this kind of fishing."

How to Call Up Smallmouth with a Spinnerbait

WORK the structure by holding your boat well away from the break and making long casts over the lip using a spinnerbait. This way, you won't spook bass in the shallows. Then turn around and cast over deep water for suspended bass.

START reeling even before the bait hits the water. Cruising smallmouth are drawn by the frantic action and often strike immediately.

RETRIEVE your spinnerbait fast enough to keep it running no more than a foot beneath the surface. Cruising smallmouth look up for their food. If you don't get a strike within the first 10 feet, quickly reel in and cast again.

How to Call Up Smallmouth with a Stickbait

MAKE a long cast to reach smallmouth that haven't been spooked by the boat; the fish seem drawn by the big splashdown.

WAIT for the ripples to subside before starting the retrieve. This gives any smallmouth in the vicinity time to swim over, inspect the bait and possibly strike it.

WALK the bait by giving it a series of rapid downward twitches. How hard you twitch determines how far the bait will veer to the side.

SWITCH to a smaller stickbait, such as a Zara Puppy, when smallmouth are making passes at the bait, but not grabbing it.

How to Call Up Smallmouth with a Minnow Plug

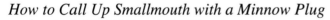

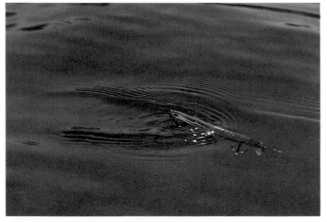

SOFTLY NUDGE the bait a few times after casting and letting the ripples subside. On each nudge, the nose of the bait should dip beneath the surface, and the tail should come out of the water. Then, rip the bait toward you; the change of speed may draw a strike.

LOOK for followers; smallmouth tend to chase minnow plugs without striking. Should you spot a fish behind your bait in the clear water, try to trigger a strike by slowing down and twitching the bait gently, so it barely moves ahead yet maintains its depth.

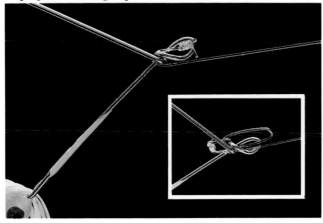

CHECK a twist-eye spinnerbait after each cast; your line will de damaged if it fouls around the arm and catches in the twist as shown. Attaching the bait with a clip (inset), minimizes damage when the line does foul.

WATCH closely when landing your fish. Clearwater smallmouth have a tendency to chase each other, possibly to steal whatever food one has captured. Even if you can't catch the followers, they tell you the spot has potential.

AVOID light-wire, R-bend spinnerbaits. Aggressive smallmouth can easily bend them, and the metal will eventually fatigue and break.

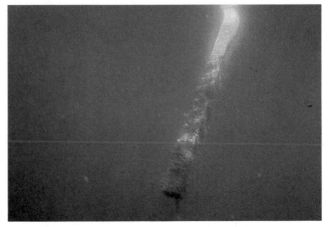

LOOK for subtle features, such as a buoy and its chain, that will attract smallmouth in open, coverless water. Even if the feature does not provide cover, it gives the fish something to which they can relate.

MODIFY a standard tandem spinnerbait (top left) to make it helicopter better. Remove the blades, cut an inch off the wire shaft, add a ball-bearing barrel swivel (arrow) and replace the blades as shown (bottom left). Reel the bait steadily, briefly stopping a couple of times during each retrieve (right) and throwing slack into the line so the bait stops abruptly and starts to helicopter. Then snap the bait back into motion and resume the retrieve. Try this change of pace when smallmouth are just nipping at the bait.

111

Thinking Light for Clearwater Smallmouth

S mall lures have long been considered the standard for clearwater smallmouth. Tiny crankbaits, ⅛- ounce jigs, 4-inch worms and small surface plugs account for a high percentage of the catch in these waters. In years past, small straight-shaft spinners would have made this list, but their popularity has waned, especially among tournament anglers.

Pros like Floyd Preas, however, know that spinners are no less effective today than they were decades ago. He has perfected a light-tackle, spinner-fishing method ideal for catching smallmouth in shallow water.

Known as the smallmouth guru on Arizona's Lake Apache, Preas has found that spinners outfish other lures during coolwater periods, assuming the water is fairly clear. Small spinners are most effective because they're about the same size as young-of-the-year shad, and they can be retrieved very slowly to tempt fish that are not feeding aggressively.

"Big smallmouth love these little spinners. It's not unusual to weigh in a 3-pound average," Preas says. "Once, while filming a TV show, I caught a 5¼- and 5½-pounder within 10 minutes of each other."

Although Preas developed his spinner-fishing method on clear canyon reservoirs, it has wide application. It's effective in any clear body of water with minimal cover, but is not a good choice for fishing heavy cover, because of the bait's exposed treble hook.

Optimal Conditions:

Type of Water: any clear lake with sparse cover
Season: mid-fall through spring
Water Temperature: 55 to 65°F
Weather: warm and sunny
Water Stage: normal, stable
Water Depth: 3 to 10 feet
Water Clarity: moderately clear to very clear
Time of Day: warmest hours, usually 10 a.m. to 4 p.m.

Floyd Preas

Hometown:
Apache Junction, Arizona
Favorite Waters for Technique:
Apache and Roosevelt lakes, Arizona; Lake Powell, Arizona/Utah
Career Highlights:
Winner: 1983 Western Bass World Team Championship; 1990 All-Star Bass Super Team Championship
One of Arizona's best-known anglers, with numerous radio and TV appearances; fishing guide for 25 years; fishing instructor and lecturer

Where to Find Coolwater Smallmouth in Clear Canyon Reservoirs

Smallmouth fishing in clear canyon reservoirs peaks in coolwater periods. Beginning in early fall, small-mouth gradually move shallower. When surface temperatures dip into the low 60s, you'll find them actively feeding at depths of 10 feet or less. Prime fall fishing continues until the temperature drops to about 50. There may be a midwinter lull, when smallmouth go deep, but the action resumes in late winter, when temperatures begin to edge above the 50-degree mark.

Start looking for fish along rocky main-lake banks and points that slope at a moderate rate into deep water. Avoid sheer cliffs at these times of year. The type of rock is also important. Look for rounded, baseball- to basketball-size rocks. They seem to hold more crayfish than the crumbly, jagged-edged shale rock.

One of the prime smallmouth-fishing areas during coolwater periods is a sun-drenched, rocky bank. Many banks in canyon reservoirs never see the sun this time of year, because it doesn't get high enough to reach them.

Smallmouth remain in these areas through spawning time, then gradually retreat to deeper water with steep-er structure, particularly bluff walls.

Not all coolwater smallmouth are found along rocky banks. A good share of the population remains at depths of 30 feet or more. These fish are much less aggressive and more difficult to catch than those in shallow water, but you can take a few by jigging vertically with a jigging spoon.

Rounded rocks (top) draw more smallmouth than jagged ones (bottom)

How to Fish Small Spinners

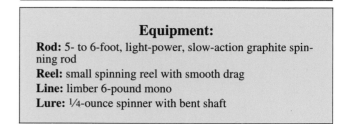

Equipment:
Rod: 5- to 6-foot, light-power, slow-action graphite spin-ning rod
Reel: small spinning reel with smooth drag
Line: limber 6-pound mono
Lure: 1/4-ounce spinner with bent shaft

Many bass anglers consider spinners to be "no-brainer" baits; all you do is blindly cast and retrieve, they say. But those who specialize in spinner fishing know there's a lot more to it.

"You can't just toss your spinner out and reel it in," says Floyd Preas. "You got to fish it." By that, he means you must keep your bait in the fish zone and work it the right way to maximize strikes.

"Got to use the right kind of spinner, too," Preas adds. "Panther Martins aren't bad, but they twist your line. Couldn't find anything that I really liked, so I started making my own and selling them. I call 'em Yellow Jackets." The purpose of the bent shaft is to eliminate line twist.

A 1/4-ounce spinner is ideal for coolwater fishing, because you can retrieve it slowly and the blade will still spin. A heavier spinner has a bigger blade, so you'd have to retrieve faster to keep the blade turn-ing. Color selection depends mainly on cloud cover and water clarity. A good all-around choice is a spin-ner with a silver blade and a red-and-yellow body. When skies are sunny and the water clear, try a gold blade and black body. When it's overcast and the water is discolored, a fluorescent-orange or char-treuse blade with a black body works better.

Casting these light baits is easiest with a slow-action rod and light line. The flexible tip lets the rod do the work so you don't have to "throw" the bait. Snags are not much of a problem, so there is really no need for heavy line.

The best way to keep your bait in the fish zone is to position your boat at the depth you expect the fish to be, and cast parallel to the bank (opposite).

The retrieve is critical. After making a long cast, allow the bait to sink; how far depends on the water depth. You want the bait close to bottom, but not bumping rocks. Then, reel slowly, occasionally stopping to let the spinner sink. This often triggers a strike. Resume your retrieve after the spinner sinks a foot or so.

On sunny days, smallmouth often hug the bank, probably because the water there is slightly warmer than the water a few feet deeper. In this situation, position your boat tight to shore and cast parallel to the bank. Don't be afraid to toss the bait within inches of shore; that's where most of the fish will be.

Strikes are usually obvious, but there are times, particularly in fall, when smallmouth tend to grab the bait and swim with it; all you feel is a deadening of the blade action. Whenever the blade stops thumping, set the hook. If a fish strikes and misses, stop your retrieve and let the bait flutter down. Many times, the bass will come back and strike again.

With tackle this light, how you set the hook is important. If you jerk too hard, you'll rip the small treble out of the fish's mouth. Instead, when you feel a strike, just raise the rod and start cranking rapidly. Keep steady tension on the fish and allow it to fight against the arched rod until it tires. Make sure your drag is set fairly loose; this way, you can't horse the

A selection of Preas' favorite bent-shaft Yellow Jackets

fish too much, and there's little chance it will break your line.

"You can call a spinner a no-brainer bait," Preas says, "but it should be a part of every smallmouth angler's bag of tricks. When you're fishing a nothin' bank, I mean a bank as smooth as a baby's butt, there's really no substitute."

Spinner-fishing Tips

CAST parallel, rather than perpendicular, to the bank when fishing a steep sloping shoreline. A parallel cast keeps the lure in productive water longer.

LOOK for trenches formed by running water. To find the trenches, look for washes along shore and scan adjacent flats with a depth finder.

MAKE your own anti-twist spinner by bending the spinner shaft as shown. The bend creates a keel effect, which keeps the bait from spinning.

APPLY a spray-on softener, such as Reel and Line Magic, to your line to keep it supple. This reduces coiling, so line flows easily off the spool, improving casting distance.

Tournament Fishing

The final weigh-in at the BASS Masters Classic is a spectacular show

Tournament-Fishing Basics

Tournament fishing is not for everyone, but if you're the competitive type, you'll probably enjoy it. Not only will you learn a great deal from experienced tournament anglers, you'll meet new friends and may even win a little money.

But don't get into tournament fishing with the idea of making a career of it; only a very few top pros could make a decent living solely from tournament winnings. Much of their income comes from product endorsements, seminars and other public appearances.

The best way to get started in tournament fishing is to join a bass-fishing club. Most of them conduct low- or no-entry-fee tournaments on close-to-home waters. After you develop confidence in your tournament-fishing skills, you may want to consider

money tournaments and statewide competition, which sometimes earns you qualifying points for national events.

There's more to tournament fishing than paying your entry fee and showing up. To be competitive, you'll have to do some research, particularly if the event will be held on an unfamiliar body of water. You need to know locations, depths, cover types and patterns that have worked well in the past. We'll show you how to gather this crucial information.

Everyone you talk to – bait-shop operators, local anglers, guides and other tournament entrants – will offer you advice on how to proceed. But the only sure way to collect reliable information is to do some pre-tournament scouting and fishing on your own. We'll give you some tips on making the most of your time.

When formulating your tournament strategy, consider the type of event you're fishing. A single-day tournament, for instance, may require a different strategy than a three-day tournament. We'll provide some recommendations for each popular tournament type.

Tournament Tips from the Pros

Regulars on the pro bass-fishing circuit know what it takes for consistent tournament success. Whether you fish tournaments for fun or have aspirations to become a professional tournament angler, it pays to heed the advice of pros who have spent many years competing at the highest level.

But don't get hooked on tournament fishing to the point where it affects your job and family life. Look at it as a competitive sport that can help you improve your fishing skills.

Shaw Grigsby

"I firmly believe that anyplace in the lake holds fish – I mean anyplace! If you only have a day or two to practice, pick out a small section of the lake, fish everything you can fish, and try to develop a pattern. Then apply it to the rest of the lake. Most people run all over the lake, trying this and that. But they never figure out what the fish are doing because they're skipping around too much."

Ken Cook

"To separate yourself from the crowd, you have to have a different mindset than the average tournament fisherman. You've got to think differently – not only about lure and presentation strategies, but also about locational patterns. I generally look at a lake map and pick out the most obvious spots. Then I avoid them, because everybody else has a map and will key on those same spots."

Jay Yelas

"It's important to gain experience by fishing a lot of small tournaments before entering the big ones. Fishing a tournament is a lot different from just going fishing. You have to learn how to deal with a partner, how to put time restrictions on your day, and all that. I see a lot of guys jumping into big tournaments too soon and they usually struggle."

Zell Rowland

"I like to figure a lake out for myself, rather than rely on information from other fishermen. I collect some basic information from local sources, like water color and type of cover and structure; then I take it from there. All a guide will do is show you the community holes and how to run the lake. I prefer to run the whole lake myself; I just take along extra props."

Mike Folkestad

"To be a successful tournament fisherman, you must have tremendous confidence in your ability and *know* you can win. The best way to build confidence is to go out by yourself and figure out a pattern on your own. Finding your own fish is a lot of work, and there'll be days when you catch nothin'. But fishing somebody else's fish won't help your confidence."

Stacey King

"It's critical to have a thorough knowledge of the bass itself and what he does year-round. A good understanding of different lake types is also important. Always remember – you'll never learn it all, so keep an open mind and try to pick up something from everyone you fish with, regardless of the level of their knowledge."

Pretournament Research

Tournament fishermen must learn to analyze information collected from many sources and weigh it in light of what they know about bass behavior in a particular body of water. They put the most stock in first-hand accounts, realizing that hearsay from tackle-shop operators, resort owners and weekend anglers could be outdated, and are skeptical of information offered by other tournament entrants, which could be intentionally misleading.

When you enter a tournament, it pays to collect the following information before you begin to practice:

Tournament rules are varied and may be complex

Tournament Rules

Obtain a copy of the tournament rules and study it before doing your on-the-water research. It may limit pretournament fishing dates and prohibit use of some techniques, such as trolling. It may also specify certain areas that are off-limits to fishing, such as fish refuges, private waters, tributaries and release sites from recent tournaments. If you are unsure of a particular rule, consult the tournament director.

Lake Information

Information from local fisheries personnel can be helpful in planning your fishing strategy. Request a contour map, and ask for other maps, which may offer different information. Obtain a copy of the latest lake survey, which usually includes information on gamefish and forage fish populations, water quality, and aquatic vegetation types in different sections of the lake. If there is more than one bass species present, get specifics on which sections of the lake are best for each. Knowing what the predominant forage fish is can be helpful in selecting baits and planning your fishing strategy. If the lake has pelagic forage, such as shad, the bass tend to move and suspend more than in lakes with nonpelagic forage.

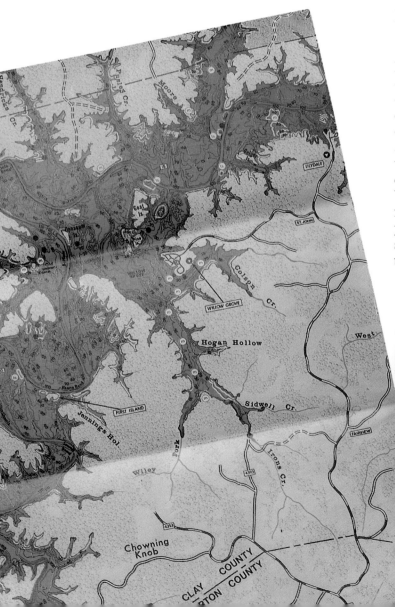

Lake maps and surveys are invaluable in planning strategy on an unfamiliar lake

Navigation Rules

Collect information on special waterway regulations, such as slow zones. You can save lots of fishing time by avoiding closed-throttle areas. Be sure to ask how water level affects access to various parts of the lake. State fisheries or reservoir personnel should have this information.

Past Tournament Results

Check results of past tournaments held on the same body of water at the same time of year. Assuming that conditions are similar this year, those results can help you determine the most productive depths, general locations, cover types, and the most effective techniques. Past results may be available from tournament organizers or from fishing newspapers or magazines.

Tournament results will also give you an idea of what species of bass is most likely to give you a win, and what the winning poundage will be. Knowing this will help you formulate an overall tournament strategy, gauge your pretournament fishing success and determine when you need to change locations or techniques.

Current Conditions

Monitoring weather conditions in the weeks before the tournament helps you determine how the season is progressing. For example, if the tournament is scheduled during what is normally the post-spawn period, but the weather has been abnormally cold, spawning will probably be delayed. This means you'll find bass farther back in creek arms or bays than you might have thought.

Before you start practicing, check the present water conditions, including temperature, flow, level and clarity. Monitor these conditions during practice and tournament fishing. Then, should conditions change, you'll have a better idea of what to do. If the water level drops, for instance, the fish will most likely go deeper; if it rises, they'll move shallower.

I★N★Bass Tournaments
Jackpot Division Results

Saturday, March 26   Grand Lake, OK

Jim Linton and Ron Walker, both from Southwest City, MO, took top honors at our Grand Lake, OK Jackpot event, held on Saturday, March 26th. On a cold, rainy day, the pair used crank baits and spinnerbaits in shallow water at the lower end of the lake to take a 6 fish limit weighing 28.44 lbs. They were awarded $1000.

Second Place went to Ken Christ of Lincoln, NE and Kurt Johnson of Norfolk, NE. They managed a 6 fish limit weighing 27.20 lbs. Their catch netted them $632. Third Place went to Lance Marshalla and Lee Wubbels, both from Lincoln, NE. They weighed in a 6 fish limit totalling 25.20 lbs., good for $457. The Big Bass of the event went to Johnny Heise and Scott Renick, both from Lincoln, NE. At 7.74 lbs., it netted them $348.

In all, 58 participating teams brought in 140 bass weighing 257.04 lbs. There were 11 - 6 fish limits. There was 100% live release.

Saturday, April 9   Fort Gibson, OK

The team of Hill & Schwartz used plastic worms on main lake points to take the win on Fort Gibson, OK on Saturday, April 9th. They weighed in 4 bass totalling 13.66 lbs., good for $500. They also had the Big Bass of the event, at 7.40 lbs.

12 teams participated in this event. There were four other tournaments on the lake, cutting our attendance significantly. 25 bass were brought in, with a total weight of 81.24 lbs. There was 100% live release.

Saturday, April 30   Smithville, MO

Fishing the main lake with crank baits, Jeff & Travis Combs, a father-son team from Friend, NE, took top honors at our Jackpot event, held at Smithville, MO in conjunction with our Regular Division event. They managed a 6 bass limit weighing 24.64 lbs., good for $670 plus another $132 for the Big Bass - 7.57 lbs. The pair also won the Regular division event, see recap of this in the Regular division section.

Second Place went to Everett & Carolyn Donham from Wichita, KS. They had 6 bass weighing 22.82 lbs. They won $400. Third Place went to David Grove - Cameron, MO & Robert Grove - Trimble, MO. They had 4 bass weighing 14.96 lbs., good for $292.

Total bass numbers, weights, etc. can be found in the Regular Division recap of this event.

Pretournament Fishing

Several rods rigged with different baits make it easy to experiment when prefishing

To have a reasonable chance of cashing, you must spend a day or two practice fishing, or "prefishing," as tournament anglers would say. In preparation for major tournaments, some top pros prefish for two weeks or more. You may want to prefish with a friend. This way, you can cover more water in less time, and experiment with more presentations.

Prefishing helps you eliminate unproductive water and zero in on the most productive areas. It also helps you determine which techniques are most likely to work in each situation, and builds up your confidence so you won't panic and prematurely start switching patterns after the tournament starts.

Another prefishing objective: become familiar enough with the body of water that you can navigate confidently and develop a feel for running times. Begin prefishing in an area known to have a high bass population. It's easiest to establish a successful pattern where there are lots of fish. Later, once you find a good pattern, you can try it in out-of-the-way places that aren't fished as heavily.

When trying to establish a pattern, keep close track of details. If you're fishing submerged timber, for example, note whether most of the fish are holding near the ends of the limbs or close to the trunk, and whether they're in the treetops or near the bottom. And try to determine how time of day, water level and weather, especially cloud cover and wind direction, affect the pattern.

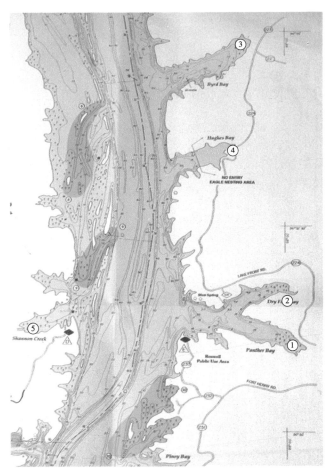

KEEP a notebook describing in detail any productive spots that you find when prefishing. Include sketched maps and landmarks, so you can quickly return to the precise spot at tournament time. It's difficult to remember all of these details when you're fishing dozens of spots every day.

EXPAND locational patterns by looking for other similar areas on a lake map. If, after thoroughly scouting a section of the lake, you found bass only around (1) submerged weeds in a deep creek arm, look for other similar areas, such as (2) and (3). Area (4) lacks weeds and area (5) is too shallow, so they would not be good choices.

To get a better idea of the exact type of structure and cover the fish are using, note the precise spot where you got a strike, then motor over and examine it. You may find a subtle depth change, a stump or a clump of weeds that you may not have noticed from a distance. Use this information to help formulate your locational pattern.

It pays to vary your bait choices and retrieve styles when prefishing. Most tournament anglers carry several rods with different baits tied on each. They experiment with different colors, sizes and types of baits, and different retrieve speeds and tempos, until they find the combination that works best for the location, time of day and weather conditions. When making bait-choice decisions, do a little research to determine what the locals have been using. It may be hard to improve on tried-and-true favorites.

But don't waste time trying to learn a completely new technique. You won't have enough time to per-

fect it, so even though it's effective for some anglers, you'll do better by sticking with familiar presentations.

When prefishing, try to identify a number of spots that are likely to produce under different wind and weather conditions. Look for some "numbers" spots and other big-fish spots. This way, you'll know right where to go should you need several small fish to stay in contention on a slow day, or one big one to register a knockout blow.

Never "burn" the fish you want to catch in the tournament. You want to get bites so you know where the fish are, and you may want to land a fish or two in each spot so you know how big they are, but you don't want to catch so many fish that you "educate" them. To ensure that you don't catch the fish, bend your hooks closed or cut them off and, instead of setting the hook when you get a strike, just try to jiggle the bait so the fish will drop it.

Give your established patterns a chance to work

Tournament Strategies

By the time tournament day arrives, the most difficult part of a tournament fisherman's job is completed. He knows what he has to do – now he must do it.

Your strategy for the day's fishing depends not only on the type of tournament, but also on the overall scope of competition. For instance, you would probably approach a tournament that is part of a total-points annual circuit differently than you would a one-time event. If you're accumulating points, it's important to register a decent weight, even if you don't win, so you should use the numbers philosophy: concentrate on catching as many fish as possible, with the idea that you'll sort out a respectable limit. But in a one-time event, you can go for broke and concentrate on big fish. If you don't catch any, all you've lost is your entry fee.

Another consideration in formulating your strategy is the bass population, itself. If the population is relatively small, the numbers philosophy is best. But if there are lots of bass and most contestants will likely catch a limit, concentrate on big fish. Your strategy will also differ depending on the length of the tournament.

The first thing to do on tournament day is to compare weather and water conditions with those encountered during prefishing. Ideally, conditions will be identical, but this is seldom the case. If conditions are similar, stick with the patterns you found. If not, you'll have to do some adjusting.

Perhaps the most common mistake, particularly among tournament-fishing novices, is to abandon their established patterns too soon. After an hour or so with no fish, they start to panic, so they scrap a proven pattern in favor of an untested one. Had they stuck with the original plan, it probably would have paid off before the day was over.

If the conditions differ from those you faced in practice, use your best judgment to come up with a new pattern. Let's say the weather during prefishing was hot and calm, and you were catching bass on topwaters in shallow weedbeds. But on tournament day, you're faced with blustery, cold-front conditions. Don't abandon your pattern completely; make some minor adjustments first. Try slowing down your retrieve a little. Or, try fishing with a bait that runs a little deeper.

Pay attention to other tournament boats. If they're moving around a lot, you can bet the bass aren't cooperating. So if you're catching a few fish, but are thinking of moving or trying something different, you may want to reconsider.

The most unnerving situation is to find another tournament boat in your prime spot. Should this happen, observe the other anglers closely to determine exactly what cover and structure they're fishing, and how they're fishing it. If their pattern is different from yours, you may be able to fish right behind them with good success. Even if it's not, it may be possible to milk a few more fish from the spot by working it more slowly and thoroughly.

Following are descriptions of the most common types of bass tournaments, and some specific tips for fishing each type:

BUDDY TOURNAMENTS. In this type of tournament, you team up with a partner of your choice. Joint decisions determine tournament strategy, including where to fish and who will run the boat. The combined weight of a team's catch determines its standing.

Here's how you can improve your success in buddy tournaments:

•Select a partner with whom you're well acquainted; this way, there are no credibility questions, and you'll be less hesitant to suggest new strategies. Avoid switching partners for every tournament. If you stick with the same partner, you'll learn to work as a team.

•Assuming both partners are competent anglers, it pays to do your prefishing separately. This way, you can cover more water and improve your team's chances of finding fish.

•The angler running the boat should plan his casts to leave plenty of good casting targets for his partner. Each angler should watch where the other is casting, to avoid covering the same water.

•If there is a shortage of good casting targets, each angler should use a different presentation, including a different retrieve angle.

•When one angler hooks a fish, the other should immediately cast to the same spot in case there's a school in the area.

•When one angler misses a fish, the other should cast to it immediately. The sooner the fish sees another bait, the more likely it is to strike again.

DRAW TOURNAMENTS. Partners are chosen by a drawing. They must make a joint decision on whose boat to use. Each operates the boat for half the day and makes the decision on where to fish dur-

ing that time. Fish weights are tallied separately for each contestant. Here are some suggestions for fishing draw tournaments:

•Each angler tends to prefer his own spots, but if your spots are far from those of your partner, you'll waste a lot of time running between them. In this case, it pays to compare fishing spots and make a joint determination on whose are most likely to yield a winning weight.

•Don't exaggerate your prefishing success to convince a partner to fish your spots. His may actually be better, and you'll both pay the price. You'll also lose the opportunity to learn something from your partner, which is one of the reasons for fishing draw tournaments. If you develop a reputation for embellishing your success, partners will not be truthful with you in future tournaments, making accurate assessment of each other's information impossible.

MULTIPLE-DAY TOURNAMENTS. Both buddy tournaments and draw tournaments can be multiple-day events. In draw tournaments, you fish with a different partner each day, and each angler's weight for each day is tallied for a tournament total. The following hints will boost your success in multiple-day tournaments:

•When prefishing, try to locate a few more spots than you would for a single-day event. The extra fishing days mean that spots are pressured more heavily, so you may not be able to catch as many fish from a single spot.

•Try to develop fall-back patterns when prefishing. With the heavy pressure, anglers soon catch the aggressive fish, but you may be able to take a few more fish from a given spot by using a presentation that's a little different. If most anglers are catching the active fish by bulging spinnerbaits over the weed-tops, for instance, try a slightly faster retrieve to make the blade break the surface.

•Work the most popular spots, or any small, isolated spots, first. By the second day of the tournament, most of the fish in these spots have been caught or at least spooked. Then, it helps to have a few less obvious spots as a fall-back.

•Assuming you're in a multiple-day draw tournament, don't hesitate to try your partner's pattern on the first day. You may be able to use it in your own spots on subsequent days.

•Should you catch a quick limit of decent fish on the first day, spend the rest of the day scouting for new spots and bigger fish. This way, other fishermen won't know where you caught your fish, and you can use the same strategy the next day without fighting a crowd.

Index

Cy DeCosse Incorporated
offers a variety of how-to books.
For information write:

Cy DeCosse Subscriber Books
5900 Green Oak Drive
Minneapolis, MN 55343